SOJOURNER TRUTH
Ain't I a Woman?

**Patricia C. McKissack
and Fredrick McKissack**

SCHOLASTIC INC.
New York Toronto London Auckland Sydney

To our sons

ISBN 0-590-44691-6

17 19 20 18   1   123/0

Printed in the U.S.A.   40

Contents

Sojourner Truth

Introduction

For the first twenty-eight years of her life, Isabella Van Wagener was a slave. But she lived as a free woman for many years after that before she decided to rename herself Sojourner Truth. By shedding her slave name, Sojourner broke all ties to her painful past and mentally claimed the freedom she had been denied at birth.

In 1850 Sojourner published her autobiography: *Narrative of Sojourner Truth: A Northern Slave.* In this detailed account of her life, Isabella the slave woman revealed the hardships of her early years and the peculiarities of Northern slavery.

Sojourner was born sometime in 1797, the same year John Adams became the second president of the United States, and George Washington warned the nation in his farewell speech that regional bickering would one day "disrupt the Union."

She was given the slave-name Isabella, but her mother and father shortened it to Belle. Belle and her parents were owned by Colonel Johannes Hardenbergh, whose family was one of the oldest and wealthiest landowners in Ulster County, New York. The Hardenberghs at one time owned nearly two million acres between the Hudson and Delaware rivers. The old manor house, Stone Ridge, was built in 1672 by Louis Hardenbergh, son of the *Espous Patroon* of Holland. The family boasted that they were the proud descendents of early Dutch settlers who had come to the New World, beginning in 1624.

By 1626 the Dutch had bought Manhattan Island from the Canarsee Indians for $24 worth of bangles and beads and had immediately begun building Fort New Amsterdam at the southern-most point of the island later known as Manhattan. That same year, the settlers brought eleven black indentured servants from the West Indies to help build their fort, which was finished in 1635.

Those first blacks who survived the brutal winters, accidents, disease, and backbreaking labor in time earned their freedom and became accepted members of the colony. Although the Dutch were vigorous slave importers, Dutch documents show that as early as 1643, a free black man, Comingo Anthoney, owned property in the area known today as Greenwich Village. At that time it was little more than a swamp. In 1647, a land grant was given to Jan Negro, an indentured servant "who came with the privateer."

While some free blacks lived, worked, and conducted business in New Amsterdam, a larger population of blacks were slaves for life, especially when the colony came under England's rule.

The English defeated the Dutch in 1664 and captured all their holdings in the New World. New Amsterdam was renamed New York and became a flourishing slave market. (It is interesting to note that slavery didn't start in the Georgia colony until 1749.) Ships loaded with human cargo found a ready market in New York harbors. Unlike the indentured servants of the past, these captive Africans were sold into a bitter life of forced labor, from which there was no hope for freedom.

By 1700 New York harbor was jammed with ships carrying human cargo. The inhumanity of the slave market led a Bostonian, Judge Samuel Sewell, to write *The Selling of Joseph*, the first anti-slavery essay written in the colonies. The frequency of slave uprisings in New York also shows how many blacks opposed slavery and fought against it.

Protests and rebellions didn't stop the ever-increasing slave trade. By 1720 there were four thousand slaves among the thirty-one thousand colonists living in New York, making it one of the largest slaveholding states north of Maryland prior to the Revolutionary War.

Most of the slaves were owned by Dutch descendents who left crowded Manhattan and pushed eighty miles upstate where they started quiet farming communities. The large estate owners, like the Southern planters, believed slavery was an essential element in a prosperous economy. They depended on cost-free labor to guarantee high profits.

But through the years, the resistance to slavery became more outspoken, especially among the New England Quakers who were appalled by the system. However, the pro-slavery forces were just as determined to maintain the status quo. Led by rich and powerful Dutch landowners like the Hardenbergs, the pro-slavery faction had managed repeatedly to delay emancipation legislation in New York and New Jersey.

After the Revolutionary War, New York abolitionists attacked slavery on a national level by pushing for an end to it in the Constitution. Slavery, they argued, would "taint the new Republic." But Southerners proved to be formidable opponents. James Madison, the "Father of the Constitution," opposed slavery. However, he compromised on the slavery issue to appease the Southern states and secure the approval of the document.

Even after the constitutional government had been established, the pro- and anti-slavery factions continued to clash. When abolitionists pushed for the end of slavery to be included within the Bill of Rights, a newly elected congressman from South Carolina defended slavery on the grounds that it was a state and not a federal issue. "Let each state determine its policies regarding slavery." Then he plunged into a ludicrous debate describing blacks as "inherently inferior beings who would be harmed by freedom." And he denounced the Quakers as "spies, traitors, pacifists, and hypocritical money grubbers."

Then, in 1793, Eli Whitney patented the cotton gin and the slavery question was moot. The gin made cotton the primary crop in the South and increased the demand for slave labor. Meanwhile, Northern resistance to slavery increased. The South countered this opposition by supporting the passage of the first Fugitive Slave Law, enacted by Congress in February 1793, making it a criminal offense to harbor runaway slaves or prevent their arrest.

There were many New York slaveholders who agreed with the South's assessment of Quakers. But the Quakers' efforts only increased. If the matter was a state issue, then they would fight in the states.

Actually, the struggle for emancipation in New York had begun as early as 1777, when John Jay tried to include an abolition clause in the New York State Constitution. The attempt failed. Every year thereafter Jay submitted the bill and the move was blocked by pro-slavery legislators, supported by large landowners.

Anti-slavery forces scored a victory in 1781 when New York recognized the contributions black men had made toward the Revolutionary War effort. Those who remained slaves were automatically freed.

At times, moderate abolitionists advocated making compromises with slave owners to achieve some of their goals, while more radical abolitionists demanded immediate and unconditional freedom. Although the means differed, the abolitionists' persistence chipped away at slavery's foundation.

Still, when little Belle was born in 1797, New York and New Jersey remained the only Northern states that still permitted slavery. Even so, the days of slavery were numbered, because it was an affront to the principles upon which the new nation was founded.

Two years after Belle was born, New York passed a law that both groups could agree upon. In 1799, the state legislature voted to gradually free slaves born after July 4, 1799 — women at age twenty-five; men at age twenty-eight.

While politicians, theologians, philosophers, and landowners debated her future, Baby Belle slept in the arms of her mother, unaware of the changes that were taking place in the world around her.

PART I
Motherless Child

Sometimes I feel like a motherless child.
Sometimes I feel like a motherless child.
Sometimes I feel like a motherless child . . .
A long way from home . . .
A long way from home . . .

True believer
A long way from home.
A long way from home.

—Negro spiritual

Chapter 1
Hardenbergh's Belle

Colonel Hardenbergh noted the birth of another slave with the same indifference he might have shown a calf or a lamb. Whenever there was a slave birth, he went to see the mother and newborn in the quarters. "She has strong arms," he told the parents in Low Dutch. "She'll be a good worker."

Although Hardenbergh spoke English when conducting business, he still preferred speaking his ancestral Dutch at home. Besides, it was easier to control slaves who couldn't communicate with the majority of the people around them. So the first language the infant heard was Dutch, the language of her master.

The child was named Isabella, a name acceptable to the master; but her parents, James and Betsey, called her Belle. Belle's father, James, was called Baumfree, a Low Dutch word that means "tree." He had been a tall and strong man, proud of his ability to do hard work. However, time had taken its toll on the big man. Belle's mother was called Mau Mau Bett. She, too, was a big, stocky woman with large hands. (In some references James is called Bomefree, and Betsey is called Ma-Ma Betts.)

Both Baumfree and Mau Mau had served Hardenbergh faithfully for many years. Belle soon learned that her father had had two other wives, but they had been sold away from him. Mau Mau Bett was much younger than Baumfree, but they loved each other; theirs was a good marriage. Although they had parented ten children, all of them had died or been sold away. Mau Mau Bett and Baumfree worried that Belle might be sold, too.

Slavery cast a long shadow over slave parents and their children. They had no control over their lives, so children were often taken and sold from their families, and their parents couldn't protect them. The best Mau Mau Bett and Baumfree could do was teach Belle how to cope with her life as it was.

Since the punishment for disobedience was often brutal, Belle's first lesson was obedience. Mau Mau Bett and Baumfree instilled in their daughter the importance of hard work, honesty, loyalty, and obedience. They also taught the child to suffer silently. "Never make a fuss in front of

the white folk," her mother said. "When you got
to cry, cry alone."

When Belle was about three, Colonel Hardenbergh died. His estate was taken over by his son,
Charles, who took his father's livestock and slaves
to the house he had recently built nearby. He had
no place for the slaves, so they lived in the cellar
of the big mansion.

Many years later, Belle shivered whenever she
remembered the cold dampness of the cellar's dirt
floors. Twelve people shared the common space
with no room for privacy. Ventilation was poor,
and lighting was even poorer since the only win-
dows were tiny slits in the wall. In the summer it
was miserably hot, humid, and smelly, so most of
the time the slaves slept outside. During the winter, they huddled together around a fire in the
middle of the room to escape the bitter cold. They
used board planks as beds. Years later, Belle remembered that, even though the cellar was terrible, she was surrounded by her parents' love, and
that had made it bearable.

Shortly after they moved to the cellar, Peter,
Belle's brother was born. Now there was someone
else to love. The children grew up listening to
their mother tell stories. Sometimes her stories
were funny, but other times they were sad. One
night Belle found her mother crying. "Why are
you crying?" Belle asked.

5th
Brought forward ————————

1 Due Bill of Cornelia Wardenbergh for
two Dollars and four Cents Dated 23d
May 1805
1 Note of Hezekiah Clark for one ————
pound ten Shillings
1 Do from Do Do for five pounds
ten Shillings Dated 13 Janry 1797
an Indorsment of 12/6 on the Same

1 Note of Isaac Burhans Junr for
one pound fifteen Shillings and
eleven pence Dated 5th Febry 1796
1 Sealed Note of John L Wardenbergh
for five pounds Dated 10th Decr 1799
with Interest
1 Note from Do for five pounds of the
Same Date with Interest   5 | 10
Cash ————————————————— 100 | —
1 Negro Slave Sam ————————   1 | —
1 Negro Wench Bett ————————   100 | —
1 Do — Do Izabella ————————   100 | —
1 Do — Boy Peet ———————— | 25
Small Scales and Weights ————

Isaac LeFever } Executors

Peter Lefever } appraisers

Lewis Hardenbergh

The Inventory Record of Charles Hardenbergh, May
12, 1808, listing his property, including Sojourner
Truth's family: Sam (her father); Bett (her mother);
Isabella (Sojourner); and Peet (her brother).

Her mother answered, "I'm groaning to think of my poor children." There had been many, but all of them had been sold. "They don't know where I be, and I don't know where they be," Mau Mau Bett said. "They look up at the stars, and I look up at the stars, but I can't tell where they be."

Then she told the story about Michael [also Michel] and Nancy, two of her older children. Mau Mau Bett's eyes were filled with a strange mixture of love, anger, and hurt as she spoke.

One morning, Michael and Nancy had awoken to the sound of sleigh bells. The children had run out into the snow to see the big horse that pulled the sleigh. Meanwhile the driver had gone inside. After a while, he had come out with Master Hardenbergh. Mau Mau Bett's worst fears had been realized. Her children had been sold. Michael and Nancy didn't know it yet. Michael saw the man pull Nancy up on the sleigh. How wonderful, the boy had thought. Nancy was getting a ride. But to the boy's horror, he saw his sister shoved into a box and the lid shut and locked.

Michael had run to hide. He cried and begged not to be taken away. But Mau Mau Bett and Baumfree had been unable to help them. "My mother mourned for her lost children all the days of her life," Belle said years later.

In 1808 Charles Hardenbergh became very ill.

NEGROES
FOR SALE.

☞Will be sold at public auction, at Spring Hill, in the County of Hempstead, on a credit of twelve months, on Friday the 28th day of this present month, 15 young and valuable Slaves, consisting of 9 superior Men & Boys, between 12 and 27 years of age, one woman about 43 years who is a good washer and cook, one woman about twenty-seven, and one very likely young woman with three children.

Also at the same time, and on the same terms, three Mules, about forty head of Cattle, plantation tools, one waggon, and a first rate Gin stand, manufactured by Pratt &Co.

Bond with two or more approved securities will be required. Sale to commence at 10 o'clock.

E. E. Hundley,
W. Robinson,
H. M. Robinson.

An advertisement for a slave auction in the state of New York.

Word spread among the slaves that he was dying. They gathered to pray for his recovery. Belle was about eleven years old when Charles Hardenbergh died. The slaves wondered what would become of them? Hardenbergh had been a fairly decent slave master who had not separated families or beat them.

That night, Mau Mau Bett and Baumfree took Peter and Belle outside. She pointed to the night sky. "Up there is where God lives," she told them. "God sees and hears you always."

In her own way, the slave mother was preparing her children for separation. "When you are beaten or cruelly treated, or fall into trouble, you must ask him for help."

A few days after Charles Hardenbergh's funeral, his property — including all his slaves — was auctioned off.

Baumfree was no longer strong like a tree; with failing sight and stooped back, he was but a shade of the man he'd been. Living in the cellar, he had contracted arthritis, which had disfigured his hands and legs.

Often slaves who outlived their usefulness were "turned out" by their masters. With no way of taking care of themselves, they soon died. At the insistence of anti-slavery groups, the New York legislature had passed a law that protected old slaves. Masters could free slaves over age fifty, provided they had a way to support themselves. But sadly very few laws are without loopholes, and the Hardenberghs found one.

Baumfree was useless to them, so they freed him. To satisfy the law, they also freed Mau Mau Bett, who was younger and still able to work. She would provide for them both. Confused and frightened, the old couple begged for mercy. Where would they go? What would they do? The Hardenbergh heirs offered them the cellar if Mau Mau Bett continued to work for the family. They had to either agree or fend for themselves in a world of English-speaking people they could not understand or speak with. Mau Mau Bett and Baumfree agreed to the terms, though it was pitiful payment for their years of service.

Meanwhile, what was going to happen to Belle and Peter? Peter was sold first to a man who didn't live in the area. Belle wanted to cry, but she stood in stony silence on the auction block, saying the Lord's Prayer over and over in her head. The auctioneer called out, "Hardenbergh's Belle, age eleven, good strong body." The child didn't know the words, but she understood their meaning. She was being sold.

At first there were no bids. Belle let her mind flirt with the possibility that she might not be bought, and that she would be allowed to stay with Mau Mau Bett and Baumfree. The auctioneer ordered Belle to turn right. She didn't understand him, so he snatched her around. "Look how tall she is, even now," he pointed out. "She'll be a big woman in maturity, have lots of children, able to do lots of work."

Still there were no buyers. Belle prayed that she wouldn't be sold. Then the auctioneer threw in a flock of sheep. "They go with the girl," he said.

John Neely (some references use "Nealy"), a storekeeper from Kingston Landing, couldn't pass up such a good bargain. He bought the girl and sheep for $100, and with a crack of the gavel the sale was finalized. Belle had a new master.

Neely figured he had made a good deal, but his wife didn't think so. "The girl can't speak English," she bellowed. "She looks strong enough, but what good is she to me? When I ask for a pot, she gives me a spoon. When I ask for a skillet, she hands me a broom."

The Neelys were recent English immigrants who had started a store and dock on Rondout Creek near Kingston, New York. Their business wasn't doing so well, and Mrs. Neely blamed the Dutch community who refused to accept them. So Belle's language infuriated Mrs. Neely, and she vented her anger toward her Dutch neighbors by attacking Belle.

Belle tried to learn English, but Mrs. Neely wasn't patient. The language sessions turned into lessons in brutality. "It was like being in a war,"

A scene from a slave auction published in the November 29, 1856, issue of The Illustrated London News.

Belle described the experience later. Mrs. Neely slapped Belle for not understanding. "I told you the word for that thing is broom! Broom! Say broom!"

One Sunday morning Mrs. Neely sent Belle out to the barn. Mr. Neely was waiting for her. He ripped Belle's shirt off, exposing her back. Then he tied rods together, heated them over a fire, and beat the girl until she fainted. Lying in the straw, soaked in her own blood, Belle wept bitterly. She'd never been beaten before, and was determined to do whatever was necessary to avoid another one.

Mrs. Neely continued to scream and yell confusing commands, but Belle had learned to cope. Mrs. Neely might not have asked her to scrub the floor, but Belle scrubbed it clean so that Mrs. Neely had no reason to complain. Slowly, Belle learned a few English words.

Belle wondered if she would ever see her family again. She was about to lose hope when, one winter evening, her father came to the Neelys'. He was old and very sick. He told her that a family by the name of Simmons had rented the Big House but had let them stay in the cellar. Mau Mau worked hard, but it was hardly enough to buy food or clothing.

Belle didn't mention her own problems. But Baumfree noticed that his child didn't have on warm clothing or shoes and that the snow was deep and cold. "My feet are so big," she said, "I can't wear Mrs. Neely's hand-me-downs."

When her father got ready to leave, he hugged her and she drew back in pain. Baumfree walked out to the gate. Belle followed, stepping in her father's large footprints. Once they were out of Mrs. Neely's sight, she showed him her blood-streaked back. Rage filled him. But the worse hurt was in his spirit. His child had been horribly beaten and he couldn't do anything about it. He had never been able to protect any of his children, but this time it would be different. Baumfree was old, crippled, and tired, but he was free. He would use his freedom to help his daughter somehow.

Before he left, Baumfree promised Belle he'd try to help her. And he did. Somehow old Baumfree convinced Martin Schryver to buy his daughter from the Neelys for $105.

Schryver was a fisherman who also owned a farm and tavern-inn on the Rondout River. Belle worked hard for him, partly because she was grateful, but mostly because she feared being beaten. Soon she learned that the Schryvers were a coarse, uneducated couple, but they weren't cruel. They spoke both Dutch and English, so that made it easier for her to communicate. Without someone yelling at her all the time, Belle learned English quickly, but it was always marked by a strong Dutch accent. During that time she picked up the

KNOW all Men by these Presents,
THAT I *Johannes Doxsteder* of *Burnetfield In the County of Albany*

For and in Consideration of the Sum of *Ninety Pounds*
Current Money of the Province of
New York to me in Hand paid at and before the Ensealing
and Delivery of these Presents, by *Jacob Cuyler*
of the City of Albany the Receipt whereof I do hereby
acknowledge, and myself to be therewith fully satisfied, contented, and
paid: HAVE Granted, Bargained, Sold, Released, and by these Presents
do fully, clearly and absolutely grant, bargin, sell and releate unto the

said Jacob Cuyler a negro Named
Har. about eighteen years old

To HAVE and to HOLD, the said *Negro Nam'd Har*
unto the said *Jacob Cuyler His Eyres*
and Executors, Administrators, and Assigns, for ever. And I the said
John Doxsteder for my Self, my Heirs, Executors and Administrators,
do covenant and agree to and with the above-named *Jacob Cuyler*

His Executors, Administrators and Assigns, to
warrant and defend the Sale of the above-named *Negro Har*

against all Persons whatsoever. IN WITNESS
whereof I have hereunto set my Hand and Seal, this *Twelveth*
Day of *October* Anno. Dom. One Tousand Seven Hundred
and Fifty *Sixty three*

Sealed and Delivered in *Johan + Doxsteder*
the Presence of Mark.

George Smith
J.H. ... Juer

Negro Slavery in New York State

A bill of sale for a negro. Price — £90. — Date Oct 12th 1763 —

A bill of sale indicating the purchase of a slave in
Albany, New York, October 12, 1763.

habit of smoking a pipe, which she enjoyed from time to time until her death.

Belle stayed with the Schryvers for about a year and a half. She grew straight and tall like her father. Her dark eyes observed everything around her with a clarity that made her seem much older than her years. She helped unload the fishing boats, ran errands, planted and hoed corn, and worked in the tavern. Her hard work was rewarded with decent food, clothing, and shelter. That was more than her parents had.

One day, Mr. Simmons came for her. Mau Mau Bett was dead. The past winter had been very hard on Belle's parents. Their food and firewood had run out and they were at the mercy of handouts. Baumfree had gone out to do a small chore for pennies. When he got back to the cellar, he'd found Mau Mau Bett in a coma. By morning she'd died.

Baumfree was grief-stricken. "I should have been the first to die. Now I'm alone," he cried. Belle mourned quietly, but the loss of her mother shattered all hopes that the family might be re-united. The fate of her father was another matter. Who was going to take care of him? How would he manage without his strong and loving wife?

Belle had to go back to the Schryvers. She prayed that God would show her a way for her to help Baumfree. While working in the tavern-inn, the girl overheard conversations about slavery, and her ears perked up whenever the topic turned to abolition. That was a new English word she'd learned. Abolitionists were people who wanted to end slavery. She didn't understand a lot about it, but if she was free, she'd go straight to Baumfree. Whoever the abolitionists were, Belle prayed that the Great God in the Sky would bless their work.

Not long afterward, Belle got the bitter message that Baumfree had starved to death. After Mau Mau Bett's death, he'd been allowed to live with two other slaves on the Hardenbergh estate. But soon these people died, too, leaving Baumfree to live in the cabin alone and too sick to care for himself. He lived his last months cold, filthy, and forgotten.

Upon hearing of the old man's death, the Hardenbergh family donated a pine box and a jug of whiskey for the mourners — their final tribute to a man who had been a faithful, kind, and honest servant.

Mau Mau Bett and Baumfree were dead. (Some references suggest that Baumfree didn't die until Belle was with Dumont, her next owner.) Peter had been sold away. Now Belle had no family. Then she remembered the Great God in the Sky and her mother's comforting promise: "God is always with you. You are never alone."

One day a short, ruddy-faced man came into the tavern. At age thirteen, Belle was already tall

THE UNITED STATES LIFE INSURANCE COMPANY

IN THE CITY OF NEW YORK.

ANNUAL PREMIUM.
$ 15.07
HOW PAYABLE.
Annually
SUM INSURED.
$ 550

THIS POLICY OF INSURANCE WITNESSETH THAT

THE UNITED STATES LIFE INSURANCE COMPANY

IN THE CITY OF NEW YORK,

In Consideration of the sum of *Fifteen* dollars and *Seven* cents, to them in hand paid by *John G. Tillmann*

and of the annual premium of *Fifteen* dollars and *Seven* cents, to be paid *in advance* on or before the *Third* day of *September* in every year during the continuance of this Policy. **Do Assure** the Life of *Charles* a slave, the property of *John G. Tillmann* of *Lexington* in the County of *Fayette* State of *Kentucky* in the amount of *Five Hundred and Fifty* dollars, for the term of *One Year* to commence on the *Third day of September* 185*2* at noon, and expire on the *Third day of September* 1853 at noon.

And the said Company do hereby **Promise and Agree**, to and with the said assured, *his* executors, administrators, and assigns, well and truly to pay, or cause to be paid, the said sum insured, to the said assured, *his* executors, administrators, or assigns, within three months after due notice, and proof of the death of the said slave *Charles*

Provided always, and it is hereby declared to be the true intent and meaning of this Policy, and the same is accepted by the assured upon these express conditions, that in case the said slave *Charles* shall die upon the seas, or shall, without the consent of this Company previously obtained and entered upon this Policy, pass beyond the limits of *Kentucky* or in case the assured shall already have any other insurance on the slave hereby assured and not notified to this Company and mentioned or endorsed on this Policy, or shall hereafter effect any other insurance upon the said slave without the Consent of this Company first obtained and entered on this Policy, or in case the said slave shall die by means of any invasion, insurrection, riot, civil commotion, or of any military or usurped power, or in case the slave shall die by his own hand, or in consequence of a duel, or by the hands of justice, or in the violation of any law of any State or of the United States, or in consequence of any extra hazardous employment, this Policy shall be void, null, and of no effect.

And it is also Understood and Agreed, to be the true intent and meaning hereof, that if the declaration made by the said *John G. Tillmann* and bearing date the *Third* day of *September* 185*2* and upon the faith of which this agreement is made, shall be found in any respect untrue, then, and in such case, this Policy shall be null and void; or in case the said *John G. Tillmann* shall not pay the said premiums as above reserved, on or before the several days herein before mentioned for the payment thereof, then and in every such case, the said Company shall not be liable to the payment of the sum insured, or any part thereof; and this Policy shall cease and determine.

And it is further agreed, that in every case where this Policy shall cease, or become or be null or void, all previous payments made thereon shall be forfeited to the said Company.

And it is hereby expressly Agreed, between the said assured and the said Company, that the said assured, for and in consideration of the premises, has waived, and hereby waives and releases to the said Company, all right and title to any mutuality or participation in the profits of the said Company.

And it is further Understood and Agreed, that the interest of the assured in this Policy is not assignable without the consent of the said Company, manifested in writing.

In Witness whereof, the said United States Life Insurance Company in the City of New-York, have, by their President and Secretary, signed and delivered this Contract, this *Third* day of *September* one thousand eight hundred and fifty *two*

John Eadie Secretary. *P. Freedom* President.

COUNTERSIGNED at .... the .... day of .... 185....

Agent.

A draft of an insurance policy, for a slave listed as
"Charles," from a New York City firm,
September 3, 1853.

and big-boned. "She'll grow to be well over six feet," Schryver said.

"I need her to help out on my farm in New Paltz," the visitor said, and he offered to buy Belle for a price three times more than what Schryver had paid for her. The Schryvers didn't really approve of slavery, and it has been suggested that they might have freed Belle when she turned eighteen. But $300 was a lot of money in those days. So the Schryvers accepted the deal and, once again, Belle was sold to a new master.

Chapter 2
Dumont's Belle

Belle's new master was John Dumont. He was pleased with Belle and wrote in his record book, dated 1810, that she was "about thirteen," but "stands nearly six feet tall."

Dumont's ten other slaves welcomed Belle to the farm. As was the custom, they gave the new slave a quick description of the new master from their point of view.

They told her John Dumont was on most accounts a decent man, not given to excessive punishment. He didn't believe in separating families and, if Belle did her work and didn't make trouble, she could expect to get along fine.

Mrs. Dumont, on the other hand, possessed a vinegary disposition and a spiteful tongue. Belle was warned to steer clear of her mistress, but that was impossible since the girl worked part-time in the Big House.

The new slave went about her work quietly, but

nothing she did seemed to please Mrs. Dumont. In most encounters with Belle, the woman was wholly hateful, and seemed to enjoy making the girl miserable. She even told the white maids that they were to "lord it over" Belle and to "grind her down." And they did their best to obey their mistress's wishes.

One of Belle's numerous duties was to wash and boil the potatoes first thing in the morning. But by the time Mrs. Dumont got to the kitchen, the potatoes were boiling in dirty water. "You didn't wash the potatoes," Mrs. Dumont scolded Belle. Knowing that she was innocent, the girl tried to explain. Her denial only angered Mrs. Dumont even more, so Belle stopped protesting and tried to find some way to prove herself.

The next day she scrubbed the potatoes harder and longer than before. Still there was dirt when Mrs. Dumont inspected the pot.

Gertrude, the Dumont's ten-year-old daughter, liked Belle. Gertrude called Belle into her room later that night. Her disposition was comparable to her father's. "I suspect Kate is at the bottom of this," she said, sharing her suspicions about one of the maids who disliked Belle. Gertrude had a plan to catch Kate doing the wicked deed. For Belle this was a first. No white person had ever offered to help her out of trouble.

True to the plan, Belle washed the potatoes and

put them in the pot to boil. Then she went out to milk the cow. As soon as Belle was gone, the hired girl came in and dumped a clump of ashes into the pot. Gertrude jumped from her hiding place. "I caught you," she said, hurrying off to tell her parents. With the help of Gertrude, Belle had been exonerated.

Belle had the body of a woman but the mind of a young girl. There was no adult in Belle's life with whom she could confide, so she made decisions and solved problems based on incorrect and incomplete information. Naturally, she made mistakes and formed opinions and beliefs that were woefully inaccurate.

It was during this time that Belle decided that Dumont was a god. She reasoned in her mind that since God knew everything, then He must know about slavery. And if God knew and didn't — or couldn't — stop slavery, then her master had to be very powerful — almost a god himself.

Belle was convinced that Dumont was an all-knowing, all-seeing god. Driven by fear, she tried to gain her master's favor, often working until she dropped from exhaustion. Convinced that Dumont knew her thoughts, Belle told him everything, even reporting the deeds of her fellow slaves as well.

Dumont often bragged that Belle could do a good family's washing in the night and be ready

An illustration of early Dutch settlers in Albany.

in the morning to go into the field, where she would do as much raking and binding as his best hands.

The other Dumont slaves grew impatient with and critical of Belle. They called her a "white folks' nigger," driving her out of their circle. They didn't understand the child's hurt and confusion.

Cato, the Dumonts' driver, took Belle aside one day. "What's the matter with you, gal? Can't you see you only hurtin' the rest of us when you work yourself to death like you doin'? Next thing we know, master'll be expectin' us all to work like that. Where'll we find time to take care of our own children then? When is old people gonna rest? Workin' hard ain't gonna free any of us. Just kill us sooner, that's all."

Belle learned through Cato, who also served as the slaves' preacher, that God didn't always answer prayers right away or stop evildoers in their tracks. "He studies on the situation, hoping the evildoers will make a change of heart and correct themselves." Slowly, Belle understood that Dumont was human after all.

If he wasn't a god, then she didn't have to be so afraid all the time. She could talk to the Great God in the Sky again without her master hearing her pleas for help and understanding. For a while that lifted the heavy burden the girl had carried for so long.

Other than the slaves on the farm, who were just beginning to trust her again, Belle had no family. Loneliness was a companion she had come to accept, until Robert came into her life.

One account says she met Robert during the time of *Pinxter*, the Dutch word for Pentecost, celebrated fifty days after Easter for a full week. The slaves were allowed a week off from work, but if they chose to work, they were paid. At Pinxter time everybody, slave and master alike, enjoyed good food, good company, and fun. There was merriment everywhere — dancing, and singing.

Belle went with Dumont's slaves to a clearing where, under a great oak, the slaves' chosen leader waited for them. He was a man of imposing height,

well over seven feet tall. They called him Prince
Gerald, for he was said to be the son of a British
soldier and an African princess from the Congo.
Known for his athletic skill, he challenged men
to contests of strength and endurance. To de-
throne Prince Gerald was the dream of most young
slaves. But for as long as Belle could remember,
no one had successfully won over Prince Gerald.

After the contests, the feasting began, followed
by endless dancing to beating drums. Couples
stomped and reeled, clapped and sang far into the
night. At dawn the weary revellers rested, but the
activities began again at dusk.

It was during Pinxter that Belle allowed herself
to be happy. There was so much joy around her
she couldn't help but participate. Robert came up
to Belle. "I am Robert," he said. And she answered, "I am Belle." Maybe it was the magic of
the festival or a sudden madness, but for Belle it
was love at first sight.

Robert and Belle probably shared a lunch of
summer sausage, gingerbread, and cider. Then
they talked and enjoyed the dancing. After Pinxter
break they continued to meet, although Robert's
master, Catlin, forbade it.

Catlin wanted Robert to marry a slave on his
farm so that the children would be his slaves, too.
If Robert married Belle, their children would belong to Dumont, the mother's owner.

It didn't matter if Robert and Belle loved each

other. Love between slaves was neither recognized nor respected and their wishes were not considered. For that matter, white couples weren't allowed to court freely, either. Most nineteenth-century marriages were arranged by the father — the master of his family.

Robert was ordered never to see Belle again because a mate had been selected for him. Robert was expected to obey, but he rebelled against his master and sneaked off as often as he could to visit Belle.

One day, Catlin and his son followed Robert and, after catching him, tied the young lover's hands and beat him mercilessly. Belle pleaded to her master for help. Uncharacteristically, Dumont broke the gentlemen's agreement between slave-holders and stopped a master from reprimanding his slave.

Dumont went one step further. He demanded that Catlin and his son get off his property. "I won't tolerate that kind of beating on this farm," he yelled angrily. "You won't kill him here!"

It wasn't the habit of most masters to kill their disobedient slaves. The purpose of a beating was to make a slave submit, stay in line, out of fear. But Dumont knew that, in a beating frenzy, masters sometimes did kill their slaves. Dumont followed them home to make sure that Robert wasn't actually killed. The beating served its purpose, and that was really all Catlin wanted.

Robert lived. When he recovered he submitted to the marriage his master had arranged.

Seeing Robert beaten in front of her, knowing his humiliation, and feeling each lash in her own heart was too much for Belle. The only way to endure the painful experience was to shut down her emotions.

Belle found a secluded spot beneath a clump of willows down by the creek that ran through Dumont's land. She retreated to this secret place to pray and sing the songs her African grandmother had taught Mau Mau Bett. In her cool, quiet place, Belle felt free to cry, and she did long and often. Then, as she'd been taught in early childhood, she dried her eyes, put away the hurt, and went back to work as usual.

Dumont thought that it was time for Belle to have a husband, too. The man picked for her was named Tom. He'd come to Dumont's farm when he had been a young man. What difference did it make if Belle and Tom didn't love each other? Dumont ordered it, so they were forced to agree.

Belle went to her master and insisted that a real preacher marry them. Jumping over a broomstick wasn't enough for her. Dumont must have seen the determination in her eyes, because he agreed. Tom and Belle were legally married.

Belle could see that at one time her husband might have been a nice-looking man, but now he was old and stooped from the drudgery of field work. Soon the young bride learned that he, too, had suffered a great loss. His love had been sold away from him years earlier.

Tom's first wife had been sold to a family in New York City. Tom had run away to find her, making his way to the city on foot. He'd even managed to stay one month with the help of free blacks who lived there. Tom never found his wife, but the slave trackers found Tom. They brought him back to Dumont. When Belle touched the scars on her husband's back, she wept softly, remembering her own beating. Over the years, the scars from their terrible whippings had healed, but they were forever fresh in their minds and hearts.

Belle and Tom loved each other in their own way. He was quiet and agreeable. Belle was caring and considerate, and they shared a common respect for each other. From their union, a daughter was born one year after they'd married. They named her Diana. Over the next ten years they had four more children.

In 1817, another law was passed freeing the slaves that had been born *before 1799*. On July 4, 1827, all slaves over age twenty-eight had to be freed. (All younger slaves had been set free by the 1799 law.) In ten years' time Belle would be free!

Many of the slaves couldn't believe it. Would they live to see it? Ten years is a long time. Who had decided on ten years? Why ten years? Why not right then? What difference would it make?

Belle was willing to accept ten more years of planting and harvesting; ten more years of carrying wood and water; ten more years of washing, cooking, and cleaning for nothing but a nasty word or a complaint as payment. Knowing that at the end of ten years she would be free made it tolerable.

If people had bothered to notice, there was a change in Belle. The very idea of freedom put a bounce in her step. She even sang while she worked, always keeping her sights on Freedom Day.

One day, Dumont approached Belle with a proposition. He complimented her on the hard work she had given him for fifteen years or more. There were two more years left before he had to free her. "I'll let you go a year earlier than the law says I have to, if you promise to work extra hard for me. Besides," he added, "I'll let Tom go free with you and you can live in the cabin I own down the road." It seemed too good to be true. And it was.

Believing fully in the integrity of her master's word, Belle accepted the offer. For several months, she put in extra-long hard hours, planting, washing, cooking, cleaning, back to the fields . . . endless hours of grueling back-breaking work.

In the spring, Belle accidentally cut her hand on a scythe. The wound didn't heal properly because she continued to use it. Although it hurt and bled frequently, she never missed a day's work. The idea of freedom kept her going. The year ended; she had fulfilled her obligation. Now it was time for her master to honor his word.

At the end of 1826, Belle waited for Dumont to free her, but he didn't say a word. Not a word! Finally, she burst into the house and confronted him. The firm set of her chin should have convinced him that Belle meant business. But with

A view of New York in 1717.

the arrogance of a slavemaster, he announced the
deal was off and dismissed her.

It is reasonable to assume that Dumont had
really planned to free Belle a year earlier as a re-
ward for hard work. But when he made the deal,
he had no way of knowing that the Hessian fly
would kill most of his crops. Facing financial ruin,
he needed all his slaves — especially Belle — to
make a new start in the spring.

It is also reasonable to believe that, had Dumont
approached Belle with the truth and asked her to
stay, they could have come to some mutual and
beneficial agreement. But Dumont chose to betray
her trust.

Standing before her master, she demanded an
answer. Why wasn't Dumont honoring his word?
After searching around for any excuse, he spied
Belle's hand. "You can't expect me to free you,"
he said. "With a hurt hand you couldn't expect
me to believe you've put in extra work."

Belle rubbed her injured hand, now stiff and
twisted. Then, suddenly all the anger went out of
her like steam escaping a tea kettle. Dumont was
a little man whose words were small and mean-
ingless. Without bothering to argue or defend her
case, Belle walked away. As far as she was concerned, she was a free woman. She wouldn't be
Dumont's Belle any longer.

Chapter 3
Free Belle!

Belle gathered her five children around her: Diana, the oldest, was twelve; then Elizabeth, Hannah, Peter, and Sophia, who was less than one year old. Belle had suffered in silence too long.

"Mr. Dumont has cheated me out of my freedom and I'll not let him get away with it. I've got to go. I can't take you with me, but I'll be back for you. One day we'll be together again."

Tom tried to convince his wife that it wasn't worth fretting about. They'd be free anyway in another year. But Belle's mind was made up. She was going to run away.

The last chore Belle did for the Dumonts was spin the harvest of sheep's wool. Meanwhile, she planned her escape. She decided to leave at dawn when it was neither dark nor light. The air was crisp and cool. She wrapped an old wool shawl over her shoulders and put all her belongings in a pillow slip. Then, taking one last look at her sleep-

ing family, she hurried away, but within seconds
she returned.

She couldn't bear to leave Sophia. Tom could
take care of the older children, but the baby was
still nursing. So, Belle quickly picked up her baby
and ran. This time she never looked back!

Once down the road, Belle realized she had run
away, but *to where*? She had no money and no
friends. What would happen to them when night-
fall came? The tiny infant grew fretful. Belle
stopped by the side of the road to nurse. It gave
her a chance to think, to make some plan.

As she prayed softly for guidance, a memory
flickered in her mind. Long ago a stranger had
stopped her on the road. He'd said, "It is not right
thee should be a slave. God does not want it."
Belle, who at the time believed Dumont was a
god, told her master about the incident. Dumont
had ordered Belle to forget the man, and obedi-
ently she had. Some years later, when she realized
that her master was not omnipotent, Belle learned
that the man's name was Levi Rowe, a Quaker
who lived down the road from the Dumont estate.
Quakers were generally very active abolitionists —
and that was a word she had never forgotten!

Belle decided to seek help from Rowe. She made
her way to his house in the early morning light.
It took him a long while to answer her knock,
because the old man was very ill. The frightened
runaway poured out her story in quick bursts of

A common occurrence of plantation life is captured in this illustration of an overseer separating a mother and child.

emotion. Levi Rowe listened patiently.

He explained that he was too ill to take her in, but gave Belle the name of another Quaker family who might be able to help. Belle hurried away with fresh hope. A few miles down the road, she came to a plain but clean farm owned by Isaac and Martha Van Wagener.

When the Van Wageners heard Belle's story they opened their house to her, offering her food and shelter. And, if she wanted, she could work for them, too.

But within hours, Dumont knocked at the Van Wageners' door. He was looking for his runaway slave and suspected that she might have sought help from a Quaker family. When he found Belle,

Dumont angrily ordered her to come back. Planting her feet firmly on the ground, she refused to
return.

Many years later, Belle described the confrontation with her master in her autobiography:

> "Well, [Belle], so you've run away from me."
> "No, I did not run away; I walked away by
> day-light, and all because you had promised me
> a year of my time."
> His reply was, "You must go back with me."
> Her decisive answer was, "No, I won't go
> back with you."
> He said, "Well, I shall take the child."

At this point, Isaac Van Wagener offered to
buy Belle for $20 and Sophia for $5. This was an
odd move, because Quakers didn't condone slavery, but Dumont accepted the deal and left in a
huff.

"Thank you, Master Van Wagener," Belle said,
addressing her new owner. But Van Wagener told
Belle that she and Sophia were free. "There is but
one master," said Van Wagener, "and He who is
your Master is my Master." (Some accounts say
that Van Wagener didn't actually free Belle, but
he allowed her to function like a free woman until
Freedom Day, when slavery officially ended in
New York state.)

Belle stayed and worked for the Van Wageners

through the winter. They were a kind and gentle couple who made Belle welcome in all ways. The couple lived simply, without a lot of frills. Often they sat for hours meditating, never saying a word.

Belle missed the constant chatter of the Dumont slave quarters, the singing and endless storytelling. While she was grateful and, to a degree, happy, she missed her children — especially when she heard that Dumont had sold her only son Peter to a Dr. Gedney, who planned to take the boy to England with him as a body servant.

She even considered going back to Dumont for the sake of her children. "Jesus stopped me," she told friends later, describing a powerful force that turned her around when she tried to leave. It was a meaningful spiritual experience for her. From that day, Belle never considered going back to her old master. Besides, Freedom Day wasn't far off.

One day, Mr. Van Wagener gave Belle some distressing news. Dr. Gedney had taken Peter as far as New York, but had gone on to England without him, after discovering the boy was too young for service. He had returned the boy to his brother, Solomon Gedney, in New Paltz, but Solomon had sold Peter to a wealthy Alabama planter named Fowler, who had just married their sister Liza [also Eliza].

When Belle found out about the sale, she hurried to the Dumonts. Once again, she confronted her old master with anger and determination. In her opinion he was partly responsible for what had happened. "Alabama is a slave-for-life state," she said angrily. "There is no way he will ever be free. If you hadn't sold him, he wouldn't be there." She begged for his help.

Mr. Dumont claimed he knew nothing about the sale of Peter. He had sold Peter to be Dr. Gedney's body servant. And that's all he knew about the situation.

Mrs. Dumont mocked Belle. "Ugh! A fine fuss to make about a little nigger! Why, haven't you as many of 'em [children] left as you can see to take care of? A pity 'tis, the niggers are not all in Guinea [Africa]!! Making such a halloo-balloo about the neighborhood; and all for a paltry nigger!"

Belle responded in a slow, deliberate manner. "I'll have my child again." And, in speaking of it later, she remembered, "Oh, my God! I know'd I'd have him agin. I was sure God would help me to get him. Why I felt so tall within — I felt as if the power of a nation was with me!"

The Dumonts refused to help Belle, so she went to Solomon Gedney's mother, but she was even less compassionate. She laughed at Belle, saying, "Is your child better than my child? My [daughter] has gone out there [Alabama], and yours has gone to live with her, to have enough of everything, and to be treated like a gentleman."

Belle's answer was filled with a combination of

sorrow, fear, and indignation. "Yes, your child has gone there, but she is married and my boy has gone as a slave, and he is too little to go so far from his mother."

Mrs. Gedney laughed and sent the distressed mother away. Belle called upon God to "show those about me that you are my Helper!"

Once more Belle was aided by Quaker abolitionists. A group of them met at the Van Wageners' place to discuss the case and decide what to do. They told her that Peter's sale was against the law, because a New York state law forbade the out-of-state sale of slaves. If found guilty, Solomon Gedney faced a fourteen-year jail sentence and/or a stiff penalty, and Peter would immediately be set free.

The Van Wageners put Belle in touch with friends in Poppletown, a short walk from Kingston, the county seat. Kingston was where she had to file a suit against Solomon Gedney, and Belle had never been that far alone. It took her the good part of a day to reach Poppletown. When she came to the Van Wageners' friends, she was tired. Her hostess graciously offered the traveler food and a clean bed to sleep in.

"I was scared," Belle remembered years later. In her own words, she had never slept in such a "nice, high, clean, white, beautiful bed." It never occurred to her that the bed was meant for her to sleep in. For a while she slept under the bed, but

The Kingston Courthouse where Sojourner Truth won her case to gain the freedom of her son Peter.

decided later to use the bed because not to do so might insult her hostess.

The next morning, the family took her to the courthouse. She was more frightened by the big building than the clean bed. But the determination to get her son back bolstered her courage. After getting directions about where to go and what to do, she managed to file a complaint against Solomon Gedney, who had sold Peter out of state.

After hearing the case, the Grand Jury decided in her favor. Esquire Chipp, the lawyer her Quaker friends had helped her hire, made out a writ. She was to take it to the constable of New Paltz. The writ ordered Solomon Gedney to appear before the court with Peter. Belle said she "trotted" the nine miles from Kingston to New Paltz.

But the constable served the papers to the wrong man, giving Solomon Gedney enough time to escape. Gedney's lawyer advised him to bring Peter back. To avoid a confrontation with the law, Solomon slipped away and headed for Mobile, Alabama, before the constable realized his error. There wasn't anything Belle could do, but wait.

Solomon Gedney returned in the spring with Peter. Belle, hearing that Gedney was back, went to his house to claim her son. "The boy is mine," he said, and slammed the door in her face.

Belle wouldn't back down. She went to Attorney Chipp. This time the writ was properly served on the right Gedney. He appeared in town and paid the $600 bond, promising to appear in court to face charges that he'd sold a child out of state. Then there was another delay.

Attorney Chipp told Belle that her case would have to wait several months for the next court session. Belle complained, but Chipp lectured her about being patient, to which Belle answered, "I cannot wait. I must have him now!" Chipp sent her away.

On the way back to the Van Wageners' house, Belle met a man on the road. He greeted her cheerfully, saying he'd heard about her case. "Have they given you back your son yet?" he asked. Belle explained her problem, adding that she didn't know what else to do.

The man pointed to a stone house nearby. "Lawyer Demain [or Romeyne] lives there. Go to him, and lay your case before him; I think he'll help you. Stick it to him. Don't give him peace till he does."

Demain agreed to take her case and promised he'd have Peter returned within twenty-four hours for a fee of $5. Sojourner's Quaker friends helped raise the money. Keeping his word, Demain went to the courthouse, but he returned quickly with bad news. Peter didn't want to be with his mother! He had reportedly fallen on his knees and begged not to be taken from his master.

The next morning all parties concerned met in the judges' chambers. "No, she's not my mother!" Peter told the judge. "How did you come by that scar on your forehead?" the judge asked. Peter answered that "Fowler's horse hove [kicked] him." What about the scar on his cheek? "That was done by running against a carriage," the boy answered.

Belle was shocked and hurt when she reached out to her son and the boy clung to Gedney's leg. "No, no," he screamed out, "I don't want to leave my master. He's so good to me."

The judge wasn't fooled by the exhibition for a minute. One look at Peter's eyes made it clear the boy was terrified by Gedney. And it was obvious his words had been carefully rehearsed.

The judge awarded the boy to his mother. Once Gedney was gone, and the boy was really sure he didn't have to go, he cautiously admitted that Belle "looked a little like his mother."

The terrible ordeal was over. Belle took her son home. That night when she was getting Peter ready for bed, she saw that his back was streaked with old and fresh wounds. "My child," she whispered. "What kind of a monster could do this to a six-year-old?"

It was then that Peter told the truth and confirmed what Belle had already suspected. "Master Gedney told me to say that I didn't know you," he said, sobbing. "He told me I'd get the worse whipping I've ever had if I didn't."

The Sojourner Truth Plaque at the County Courthhouse, Kingston, New York, marks the event where Truth won a lawsuit saving her son from slavery in Alabama.

Belle held her son in her arms. "You're free now and safe with me." She was sure the man on the road who had told her about lawyer Demain had been an angel from heaven. She thanked God for helping.

It didn't seem important then, but Belle was one of the first black women in the country to win a court case. All that mattered at the time was her son. And God willing, she prayed, "no child of mine will be sold away from me again!"

Chapter 4
The Kingdom

For a while, Belle stayed in Kingston where she found work with the Latin family. Peter stayed with her, but Sophia, who was about two years old, went to live with Diana, Hannah, and Elizabeth, who all still lived and worked at the Dumont place.

Tom was freed on July 4, 1828, along with all the other adult slaves in the state. Since Belle was in Kingston at the time, and Tom was in New Paltz, it was impossible to build a home together. In time they grew apart. As they had consented out of respect to marry, they agreed for the same reason to separate. Tom did a few odd jobs until his health failed and he died before the year ended.

While in Kingston, Belle did laundry for one of Solomon Gedney's relatives. One day, while she was hanging out the wash, she heard a scream from the house. Inside, she overheard a letter being read from Alabama authorities.

Eliza Fowler had been beaten to death by her husband! The letter said he had gone mad. "How long Fowler had been insane, we don't know. Nor what she had had to suffer at his hands before . . . He's been locked up now and will be for the rest of his unhappy life, where he can do no more harm."

When Belle had seen the scars on Peter's back, she'd asked, "Was there anybody that reached out to help you, boy?" And he had answered, "Oh, mammy . . . sometimes I crawled under the stoop, the blood running all about me, and my back would stick to the boards; and sometimes Miz Eliza would come an grease my sores, when all were abed and sleep."

Seeing her child so horribly scarred, Belle had prayed, "God, render unto them who have done this thing double!" But hearing what had happened to Eliza Fowler, Belle felt hurt — responsible somehow. "Oh, my God! That's too much," she said. "I did not mean quite so much, God!"

Belle left Kingston soon after that. Her dream was to bring all her children together under one roof, but for now the best she could do was find work near them. Fortunately, the Van Wageners welcomed her back and she continued to work for them. She and Dumont had settled their differences, too, and Belle visited her daughters regularly.

Living and working with the Van Wageners was the happiest and most peaceful time in Belle's life. At night, when the chores were finished, Mr. Van Wagener read the Bible, which made so many things about God and his relationship to humans clearer to Belle. Of that time she said later, "Oh, everything [at the Van Wageners'] was so pleasant, and kind, and good, and all so comfortable; enough of everything; indeed, it was beautiful!"

In the meantime Peter's body had healed, but he still needed a lot of emotional healing. Nevertheless he was a happy child who enjoyed running and playing along the wharves in New Paltz. The ships excited him and so did the stories the sailors told. But the boy's behavior troubled his mother.

Peter began to steal; then he lied about it when he was caught. Belle was lenient with him because of his experiences, but she felt that she needed help with Peter. For a while she placed the boy with a man who worked the locks on Rondout Creek. This, she hoped, would keep Peter constructively occupied and out of trouble. Instead it got worse. Then Belle decided to seek a church home — a place where Peter could be given proper religious instruction. Maybe then he wouldn't stray from his mother's teachings.

A new Methodist Church had opened in New Paltz. One Sunday morning Belle dressed Peter and put on the one good black dress she owned.

Neither of them had shoes, but did that matter to
God? Mother and son walked to church.

At first Belle was too afraid to go inside. Only
whites were worshipping there. She loved the
hymn they were singing:

> There is a holy city
> A world of light above
> Above the starry regions,
> Built by the God of Love.

Should she go inside? Belle wondered. Then she
remembered a scripture passage from I Chronicles
29: 15–16 that said: "For we are strangers before
thee, and sojourners, as were all our fathers. . . .
O Lord our God, all this store that we have prepared to build thee a house for thine holy name
cometh of thine hand and is all thine own." Much
to her satisfaction she and Peter were accepted as
members.

During one of the services, Belle met Miss Geer
[or Gear], a schoolteacher from New York City
who was vacationing in Ulster County. Miss Geer
liked Belle but, more importantly, she was impressed with Peter's bright and inquisitive nature.
The woman told Belle about the availability of
jobs in New York and the numerous educational
opportunities for Peter.

The idea that she could *leave* was a kind of

awakening for Belle. After Freedom Day, many former slaves had gone to New York City. Others had taken work on the Erie Canal, or found jobs in Rochester, Buffalo, or Syracuse. She, too, could go to another city and find work. Why not New York City?

The suggestion Miss Geer had made seemed practical to Belle. Jobs were plentiful in the city and the pay was better. Perhaps she might be able to save enough to prepare a home for the girls, once they reached twenty-one and were freed by Dumont.

What did her children think? She talked it over with Diana, Hannah, and Elizabeth. They encouraged her to take the opportunity for Peter's sake. They promised to take care of their little sister Sophia. Even Dumont agreed with the arrangement. It felt nice to make a decision about her life without needing permission from a master.

So by the end of summer 1829, Belle and Peter left New Paltz. After a tearful good-bye with her daughters and promises to keep in touch with the Van Wageners, Belle and Peter took a boat down the Hudson to New York City. In late summer, the valley was a magnificent tapestry done in shades of plush greens. Later she realized how much she missed the rich green Hudson Valley, but for her it would never be home again.

Standing six feet tall, dressed in a plain gray

A view of the historic Hudson Valley.

dress, with a white bandanna tied around her head, Belle must have been an imposing figure. She had the cobbler make her the first pair of shoes she'd ever owned. Most of the time she went barefooted, or wore men's boots, because her feet were size twelve.

Miss Geer met them at the docks with a carriage. The New York that Belle saw in 1829 was smaller than it is today but every bit as crowded and busy. As the carriage rolled over the cobblestones, Belle clung to Peter, whose happy eyes danced from one interesting thing to another.

Sitting bolt-straight, Belle was a striking picture of composure. But, in reality, she was scared witless. The unfamiliar sights, combined with the noise and clutter, bombarded her senses and confused her reasoning. And the people! She'd never seen so many people, moving, constantly moving. Some crossing the street. Some riding in carriages with nervous horses. While still others stood around talking on street corners. It made her dizzy to look up at buildings several stories high.

Miss Geer had arranged for Belle to work for the Whitings, the Gatfield family, and then later a prominent newspaper family. And Peter was enrolled at a navigation school.

In time, Belle learned the city by wandering around the neighborhoods, looking, listening, and talking to people in shops and markets.

Five Points was the poorest section of town. Murderers, prostitutes, and thieves lived alongside widowed mothers with children and people just down on their luck.

Then there were the thousands of Irish immigrants who flooded into the city almost daily. A great many of the new arrivals didn't have jobs, so they lived in crowded, filthy conditions, unmatched even by Hardenbergh's cellar. How could free people choose to live this way, Belle wondered?

Belle soon learned that there was a longstanding free black community in New York, and she was proud to be a part of their swelling ranks.

After being told that whites and blacks worshipped in separate services at the Methodist Church on John Street, she soon found her way to Mother Zion African Methodist Episcopal Church.

It pleased Belle to know that the AME Church was the oldest African-American organization in the country. It had been started in 1787 by Richard Allen and Absalom Jones, after blacks had been denied the right to worship with white members at St. George's Church in Philadelphia. Allen, who had been born a slave in Delaware and ordained a minister in 1799, withdrew his membership and started the African Methodist Church. In 1817, he became its first bishop. And it pleased

A street scene of Broadway in New York City in the early 1800's.

Belle very much to know that, in 1824, Allen had ordained a woman, Jarena Lee. She had even preached at Mother Zion's in New York. Belle remained a beloved member of the AME Church while in New York, known for her spirit-filled prayers and original hymns.

One Sunday a man and woman approached Belle after services. "I am your sister Sophia," the woman said, "and this is your brother Michael. We are the children of Mau Mau Bett and Baum-free, too. We were told by friends that you worshipped in this church, so we came to find you."

The three of them spent the whole day talking. Sophia, she learned, was living in Newburgh and Michael, the boy in Mau Mau Bett's story, had moved to New York. Belle wanted to know what had become of Nancy, the sister who had been taken away on the sleigh with him. Michael reported that Nancy had lived in the city and attended Mother Zion until her recent death. When he described Nancy, Belle shrieked in surprise. She knew the woman as one of the elderly mothers of the church. They had prayed beside each other at the altar and sung hymns together. They never knew they were sisters.

"Here she was," Belle told her biographer with tears streaming down her face. "We met, and was I not, at the time, struck with the peculiar feeling of her hand — the bony hardness so just like mine? And yet, I could not know she was my sister; and now I see she looked so like my mother."

Belle wept and so did Michael and Sophia. "What is this slavery," Belle asked, "that it can do such dreadful things?"

Miss Geer stayed in touch with Belle and invited her to join an evangelists' group that took religion into poverty-stricken areas like Five Points, where filth and disease were as villainous as crime. Belle didn't see much point in Miss Geer and her Sunday disciples greeting people on street corners and singing hymns. These people needed food, decent houses, and warm clothing.

So, Belle offered to help out at the Magdalene Asylum, a shelter for homeless women. The big gray house on Bowery Hill was run by Elijah Pierson, a religious charlatan — but neither Belle nor any of his followers knew it at the time.

Pierson claimed he ran Magdalene Asylum "with direct instructions from God." That wasn't hard for Belle to believe. She, too, felt that God personally directed her life. Belle liked Pierson, and agreed to work part-time for him, often staying on to participate in religious services.

One Sunday Belle answered the door at the Magdalene Asylum. A strange man with piercing eyes announced himself as Robert Matthews, known better as Matthias. Belle thought he might be an angel, but he was actually a middle-aged hustler who had left his wife and children upstate

THE PROPHET!

A

FULL AND ACCURATE REPORT

OF THE

JUDICIAL PROCEEDINGS

IN THE

EXTRAORDINARY AND HIGHLY INTERESTING CASE

OF

MATTHEWS, *alias* MATTHIAS,

CHARGED WITH HAVING

Swindled Mr. B. H. Folger,

OF THE CITY OF NEW-YORK,

OUT OF CONSIDERABLE PROPERTY;

WITH THE

Speeches of Counsel, and Opinion of the Court on the motion of the District Attorney, that a Nolle Prosequi be entered in the Case.

ALSO,

A Sketch of the Impostor's Character,

And a detailed History of his Career as a "Prophet," together with many other Particulars, which have not hitherto been published.

BY W. E. DRAKE, CONGRESSIONAL AND LAW REPORTER.

NEW-YORK: PRINTED AND PUBLISHED BY W. MITCHELL, 265 BOWERY,
And may be had of him, and all the Booksellers.

1834.

Price Six Cents.

The title page from "The Prophet . . . ," an account of Matthias, written by Benjamin Folger, a former Kingdom member who accused Truth of witchcraft.

and come to the city with a new scheme. Of
course, no one knew the extent of his deceit,
either.

Within months Pierson and Matthias were part-
ners in a wickedly devised scam. The two men
were claiming that Pierson was John the Baptist
and Matthias was God on earth. "Ours is the mus-
tard seed kingdom," Matthias preached, "which
is to spread over the earth. Our creed is truth. But
no man can find truth unless he comes clean into
the church."

Words like that convinced Belle that these two
men were who they said they were. So she joined
the community known as "The Kingdom." They
organized and were headquartered upstate in Sing
Sing, New York, where all the members donated
their money and worldly possessions. Pierson and
Matthias managed all the financial affairs without
any accounting. Since Belle didn't have a lot of
money, she was accepted on the basis that she
would do the washing, ironing, cooking, and
cleaning, for the privilege of worshipping with
them. Blinded by her complete trust in these men,
Belle agreed to the terms.

As the months dragged on, however, she realized Matthias and Pierson weren't deserving of her
trust and confidence. She couldn't prove they were
dishonest, but she wanted no part of their hoax.
She prepared to leave.

First she went back to the city where Miss Geer

A record of the date Truth said she had found Jesus as the risen Savior.

helped her get her old job back with the Whitings. At that time, she learned that Peter was in trouble again. He had dropped out of school and had hired out as a coachman for one of Miss Geer's friends — but he was running around with a rough crowd. This further motivated Belle to cut her ties with The Kingdom.

When she returned to get her belongings and to serve notice, Matthias was away. Suddenly, Pierson stiffened and collapsed on the floor. He was dead by morning.

Matthias was accused of poisoning Pierson. And the trial turned into a media circus. The newspapers featured story after story about the strange religious community and the two leaders who had

used the money to fulfill their own greedy desires.
As the reports of the members' bizarre worship
practices filled the pages of the newspapers, Belle
felt hurt and betrayed. She was as shocked as anyone about the wife-swapping, communal bathing,
and extortion that were going on around her. But
the fact that she was the only black woman in
The Kingdom added drama to the newspaper accounts. Much to Belle's dismay, the public found
it hard to believe she was ignorant of the whole
sordid affair, when in fact she had been.

The trial dragged on for months. Finally, a judge
ruled that no murder had taken place. Pierson had
died of indigestion after eating too many half-ripe
blackberries. Matthias was freed. Discredited and
shown up for the rascal he really was, he left for
the West and fresh territory to exploit. But it
wasn't over for Belle.

Benjamin and Ann Folgers, members of The
Kingdom, wrote a novel in which they blamed a
maid for being the culprit who had brought evil
into a holy community. In this fictionalized account, based loosely on fact, the Folgers even described how the "black witch" had murdered the
leader of this fictional group and described in mor-
bid detail how the deed was done. People foolishly
read the novel and believed it was about Belle.
Newspapers printed the Folgers' story, making it
available to people who hadn't read the book.

Gilbert Vale was a friend of Belle's employer,

Mr. Whiting. Both men were journalists. Whiting was convinced that Belle was incapable of doing the heinous crimes the Folgers had described. He convinced Vale to take up Belle's cause, which he did.

In 1835, Vale published a pamphlet titled, *Fanaticism: Its Source and Influence, Illustrated by the Simple Narrative of Isabella*. In it Belle got to tell her side of the story. Vale wrote in the introduction that she "had shrewd common sense, energetic manners, and apparently despises artifice."

Vale suggested that Belle might sue the Folgers and the newspaper that had printed the scandalous novel implicating that she was a murderer. She knew the power of truth in a courtroom, so she accepted the challenge. This time she fought to protect the only thing a poor person has of value — his or her good name.

Belle's strategy was simple. She went back to New Paltz and Kingston and gathered character statements from her employers — even her old master.

John Dumont praised her for being "perfectly honest." Isaac Van Wagener said Belle "was a faithful servant, honest, and industrious." And her most recent employer, Mrs. Whiting, wrote a glowing report: "I do state unequivocally that we never have had a servant that did all her work so faithfully, and one in whom we could place such implicit confidence. In fact, we did, and do still believe her to be a woman of extraordinary moral purity."

Belle won her case, and the court awarded her $125 damages. All she could think of was how much time she had wasted — from 1832, when Matthias and Pierson had started the commune, to the end of the ordeal in 1835.

But they weren't really wasted years. Belle grew from the experience. Though she would have rather it not have happened at all, it was behind her now. She would never again be so easily taken in by fast-talkers who mistook honesty and sincerity for weakness.

Chapter 5
Gone Forever

While Belle was fighting to save her reputation, Peter had, in his mother's words, "gone to seed." For a while, Belle was able to keep him in line with firm discipline, but while she was away, he had dropped out of navigation school and refused to attend regular grammar school, either.

He was restless and reckless, so a city bursting at the seams with violence seemed adventuresome to a young boy. All he wanted to do was hang around with his friends who were mostly street thugs. Peter was only eleven, but he was lanky for his age, so the boys took him in. He liked being accepted by older boys, and foolishly stole things to win their approval.

Since he didn't go to school, Belle insisted that he find work. The boy had been working as a coachman for a Mr. Jones, when one day he disappeared with his employer's best saddle. He

showed up a few days later after he'd sold the saddle
and used the money having a good time with his
friends.

Mr. Jones didn't press charges, because Belle
and Miss Geer pleaded for him, but Peter was fired.
Peter flashed his charming smile, promised never
to do wrong again and all was forgotten and for-
given, for a day or two.

The Irish and blacks in the city competed for
jobs during the day, and ethnic gangs fought in
the streets for territorial control at night. Peter
often got in fights and came home for Belle to
patch him up. Belle would lecture and scold, and
Peter would plead for one more chance to make
up for his wrongdoings. But the result was always
the same; within the week, Peter was in trouble
again.

As expected, the boy got into serious trouble
with the police. Belle asked for advances on her
salary two times so she could bail Peter out of jail.
A mother's love is enduring. Once again, Belle
refused to give up on the boy. She found a job for
him at a livery stable. All he had to do was tend
the stock, rake the stalls, and clean the harnesses
and bridles. He didn't go to work half the time,
and when he did, he didn't get along with his
boss. So when Peter stole a harness and sold it on
the street, the owner was not willing to show any
mercy. He pressed charges.

Belle realized she had lost control. Peter was on a collision course with disaster, and she couldn't help him unless he wanted to help himself. So, this time, when the messenger came to tell Belle that Peter was in the infamous Tombs, New York's dreaded jailhouse, she refused to help. Having warned him repeatedly, Belle "gave him up to God."

Peter didn't believe that his mother would leave him in prison. She had *always* been there for him. When a day passed and she hadn't come, Peter got frightened. Then he devised a clever plan. Sometimes he went by the name Peter Williams. There was a preacher in town with the same name, so Peter sent for him, asking his "namesake" for help. (Some documents state that Peter Williams was a barber as well as a minister.)

Oddly, the elder Williams came to Peter's aid, but first he stopped to speak with Belle. Together they decided that Peter needed discipline — the kind he would get at sea. The judge agreed.

Peter signed as a crew member aboard the *Zone of Nantucket*, in August of 1839. A year later, Belle got a letter from him. Mrs. Whiting read it for her.

My dear and beloved Mother,
I take this opportunity to write to you and inform
you that I am well and in hopes for to find

*you the same. I am got on board the same un-
lucky ship Zone of Nantucket. I am sorry for
to say that I have been punished once severely,
for shoving my head in the fire for other folks. I
would like to know how my sisters are. I wish
you would write me an answer as soon as possible.
I am your son that is so far from your home in
the wide briny ocean. Mother, I hope you do not
forget me, your dear and only son. I hope you
all will forgive me for all that I have done.*

> *Your son,*
> *Peter Van Wagener*

Belle wanted to write Peter a cheerful letter.
(She dictated her letters and someone else wrote
them for her.) Exactly what she wrote about is
unknown, but she probably included things about
family, friends, and what was going on in the community. A lot had happened since he'd left New
York.

In 1830, there were 13,976 blacks living in the
city. Although blacks and whites worked together
to end slavery, at other times they competed vi-
olently for jobs, housing, and education. The city
government was corrupt, and crime was rampant.
It led Belle to say, "The rich rob the poor and the
poor rob one another." Many of Peter's friends
were in jail or dead. She thanked God that her
son had, so far, escaped that fate.

Belle didn't want to write Peter about the ugly side of New York. He'd seen enough of that while he was living there. She probably reminded Peter of the well-known free West Indian, Samuel Fraunces, who had owned a small tavern on Pearl and Broad Streets. Although Fraunces was dead, his place was still a favorite meeting place for New Yorkers. New York's revolutionaries had met there, and, after the war, General George Washington had said farewell to his officers in the Long Room. When Washington was elected president, Fraunces had served as steward of the presidential mansion, which was in New York at the time.

Belle greatly admired President George Washington. So, no doubt, she would have told Peter that old Mary Washington, a servant of President Washington, was still selling fruits and vegetables at 79 John Street between Gold and Nassau Street. Since Washington's death in 1799, Mary had put out a display in memory of the first president of the United States. She wanted his birthday to be a national holiday. Belle agreed.

Belle missed her son deeply, and she watched for his letters. A second letter came and five months later a third and final one arrived on September 19, 1841. He said his ship had fallen upon bad luck. But his luck was sure to change

This is the fifth letter that I have wrote to you and have received no answer and it

Samuel Fraunces, owner of the Fraunces Tavern. Located in lower Manhattan, the tavern served as a meeting place for revolutionary forces.

Fraunces Tavern.

makes me very uneasy. So pray write as quick
as you can.

Belle had only received three letters, and she
had written him many times. Why hadn't he gotten at least one of her letters?
Mrs. Whiting read on.

[I should] be home in fifteen months. I have not
much to say, but tell me if you have been up
home since I left or not. I want to know what
sort of a time is at home. So write as soon as you
can, won't you?

Peter concluded with a poem, one he found or
perhaps he wrote.

Notice when this you see, remember me, and
     place me in your mind.

Get me to my home, that's in the far distant west,
To the scenes of my childhood, that I like the best;
There the tall cedars grow, and the bright waters
     flow,
Where my parents will greet me, white man, let
     me go!

Let me go to the spot where the cataract
plays,

Where oft I have sported in my boyish days;
And there is my poor mother, whose heart ever
   flows,
At the sight of her poor child, to her let me
   go . . .
          let me go!

                              Your only son,
                              Peter Van Wagener

Belle wrote back immediately, telling Peter
about her dream to rent a house for all the family
to share. Months passed, but no letter came. Years
later, she was told that the *Zone* had returned to
New York Harbor, but no seaman by the name of
Peter Williams or Peter Van Wagener was on-
board. She remembered Mau Mau Bett's words:
"Those are the same stars, and that is the same moon,
that look down upon your brothers and sisters, and
which they see as they look up at them, though they
are ever so far away from us, and each other."
   Belle never heard from her son again, but she
kept his letters with her always. "He is good now,
I have no doubt," she told her biographer. "I feel
sure that he has persevered, and kept the resolve
he made before he left home."
   Belle often looked at the night sky and wondered if her children were seeing the beautiful
North Star. The North Star, however, had a different meaning for runaway slaves. The North Star
pointed to freedom.

In the 1830s, New York was a center for the abolitionist movement, especially among the free blacks. One of the strongest activities of the anti-slavery movement was management of the Underground Railroad. This is the way it worked.

Slaves who wanted to run away were contacted by a "conductor" who would give them directions or lead them to "stations" or safe houses along the way. There the runaways would be given food, clothing, and shelter. In this way, runaway slaves inched their way from slavery to a free state or to Canada. Songs were used to pass coded messages, and the North Star was used as a guiding light.

The "grand station" of the Underground Railroad was located in New York. David Ruggles, a

This abolitionist broadside, published by the Anti-Slavery Office of New York, was printed with John Greenleaf Whittier's poem "My Countrymen in Chains." Underneath the print appeared the words: "He that stealeth a man and selleth him, or if he be found in his hand, he shall surely be put to death."

well-known author and abolitionist, was the conductor who greeted a young runaway slave who
knocked at his door Tuesday morning, September
4, 1838.

The tall young man with dark eyes, dressed in
a borrowed sailor's uniform, said his name was
Frederick Augustus Washington Bailey. Frederick
had just arrived in New York from Baltimore, having escaped by using a friend's free papers.

Ruggles welcomed the young man into his house
at 36 Lispernard Street and gave him food and a
warm bed in which to sleep. But the young man
couldn't sleep. He was too excited. He was free
and immediately sent to Baltimore for his bride-
to-be, Anna Murray, who was a free black woman.

At that time, Reverend J.W.C. Pennington was
the pastor of the First Presbyterian Church at the
corners of Prince and Marion Street, and a leading
abolitionist. He, too, was a runaway, but had
earned a doctorate of divinity from Heidelberg
University in Germany.

Reverend Pennington married Frederick and
Anna and the couple moved to New Bedford, Massachusetts, where Frederick changed his last name
to Douglass.

Belle didn't know Ruggles or Douglass at the
time, but the three of them were traveling along
paths that would intersect.

Nine years passed in a never-ending cycle of
days followed by nights. Soon it was 1843. Belle's

Rev. James W.C. Pennington, pastor of the First Presbyterian Church of New York City, was born a slave in Maryland. He later escaped to New York and was educated in Germany.

daughters had grown up, married, and started families of their own. It saddened Belle that she hadn't gotten to spend much time with them. There wasn't much she could do about the past, so she concentrated on the future. She examined her life and wondered how she might make it better.

Then, during one of her times of deep prayer, she thought she got a message from God. "Go East." The words troubled her. "Go East." Then she decided to follow the words and "Go East," wherever it led.

Early the next morning she gave notice to Mrs. Whiting, who declared Belle crazy and protested her leaving. But the housekeeper could not be stopped. "I'm going to find a new home . . . and

A young Frederick Douglass with an excerpt from his journal describing his journey to New York City and freedom.

with a new name. I'm gone forever!"

Belle was about forty-six years old when she left New York, on June 1, 1843. She walked down to the ferry where she paid twenty-five cents for the crossing. And in her customary style, she never looked back.

By evening she was well out of the city. Stopping at a Quaker farm, she asked for a drink of water. The woman gave it to her, asking her name.

"My name is Sojourner," Belle said, no doubt remembering II John: 1–4. *"It has given me great joy to find some of your children walking in the truth just as the father commanded us."*

"What is your last name?" the woman asked.

Sojourner didn't know what to say. All her life she'd been Hardenbergh's Belle, Dumont's Belle, always her master's names. Then the thought came beautifully complete. "The only master I have now is God and His name is Truth." So she gave herself the last name Truth.

"Sojourner Truth is my name," she answered, adding, "because from this day I will walk in the light of His truth."

PART II
Truth Is My Name

I know I've been changed.
I know I've been changed.
I know I've been changed.
The angels in Heaven have changed my name.

I told the Lord if He'd take my heart —
> *The angels in Heaven have changed my name.*
I wouldn't desert when the battle got hot —
> *The angels in Heaven have changed my name.*

'Way down about the Jordan Stream —
> *The angels in Heaven have changed my name.*
I heard a cry, I've been redeemed —
> *The angels in heaven have changed my name.*

It makes me happy when I sing —
> *The angels in Heaven have changed my name.*
To know that I have been born again —
> *The angels in Heaven have changed my name.*
> > *—traditional AME spiritual*

Chapter 6
A New Direction

Sojourner walked as far as she could in one day, then found food and shelter for the night wherever she happened to be.

Just as the sun was setting on her first day out of New York, Sojourner was praying, asking God which way she should go. Suddenly, a stranger stopped Sojourner on the road and asked if she needed a job. "I'm on my way to do the Lord's work," she said, although she wasn't clear about the details of how.

The man invited Sojourner to stay at his house for the night and she agreed. Once at the farmer's house, she realized he really did need help. His wife was very ill. Sojourner stayed with the family for several weeks, nursing the sick woman, washing, cooking, and cleaning for the family. They begged her to stay, but Sojourner knew, like her

name implied, she couldn't stay any place too
long. Early the next morning, she accepted
twenty-five cents as payment and moved on.

This would be the pattern of her life for several
months. But was it for this the Lord had told her
to "go East"? One evening Sojourner came to a
large outdoor religious meeting. Hundreds of families were camped in wagons and tents. She stayed
the night and all the next day. The people ate,
sang, prayed, and listened to speakers. The at-
mosphere reminded Sojourner of Pinxter. Everybody seemed so happy, yet pious.

Sojourner, dressed in her black Quaker dress and
white shawl, approached the group and asked if
she might speak to them. She mounted the plat-
form. People gathered to hear the speaker, for they
weren't accustomed to being addressed by a black
woman. Curiosity quieted the crowd. Sojourner
presented herself well, a handsome woman,
strong-boned, and proud. Clearly she was no or-
dinary woman.

"Well, Children," Sojourner began in a deep
melodious voice. "I speaks to God and God speaks
to me." A murmur drifted through the gathering.
Standing there in the last afternoon sunshine,
talking about God's glory, love, and protection,
the African woman must have looked other-
worldly.

She ended with a hymn.

In my trials — Lord walk with me.
In my trials — Lord walk with me.
When my heart is almost breaking
Lord walk with me . . .

The group sang along with her and begged for another song when she finished. Sojourner's encore was a song she had learned from blacks who had come to New York from the South:

Sometimes I feel like a motherless child.
Sometimes I feel like a motherless child.
Sometimes I feel like a motherless child . . .
A long way from home . . .
A long way from home . . .

After that, Sojourner traveled from meeting to meeting. Once someone asked her to talk about her life as a slave. She'd never spoken in front of so many white people before, but after saying a prayer she sang a hymn, then began speaking.

"Children, slavery is a evil thing. They sell children away from their mothers, then dare the mothers to cry. What manner of men can do such a thing?"

Heads nodded in agreement, but they stayed quiet and listened respectfully.

"My mother and father had eleven other children besides me. Some of my brothers and sisters

I've never known. They were sold off before I was even born. But my poor Mau Mau Bett never stopped crying for them."

Sojourner held the audience captive as she told them the story of her brother and sister who had been sold by the Hardenberghs.

Soon word spread that Sojourner Truth was a stirring and inspirational speaker. When she came into a camp meeting, people rushed to greet her; and after hearing her speak, people were so filled with emotion that they often cheered and cried.

At first, Sojourner was taken with the notion that whites would sit still and listen to anything she had to say. Later, her goal became clearer. All her life Sojourner had been a victim of oppression, despised because of her race, and disregarded because of her sex. It was out of the fog of this life that she emerged at age forty-six, dedicated to the elimination of human suffering. She would speak out against slavery!

But Sojourner learned quickly that not all audiences were going to be considerate and receptive to her message. Once she was at a camp meeting that was interrupted by a rowdy group of young men, carrying clubs and sticks. She ran and hid in a tent behind a trunk. But she quickly regained her confidence, went out, and boldly faced the mob. By calmly taking control of the explosive situation, she convinced the men to peacefully disperse. After that incident, Sojourner never again ran away in fear.

"God's mercy will be shown to those who show mercy," summarized the theme of her speeches at this time. Listeners marveled that this woman couldn't read, yet she could flawlessly quote scripture word for word and apply it appropriately. She had memorized most of the Bible by simply listening to it.

The simplicity of her language and the sincerity of her message, combined with the courage of her convictions, made Sojourner a sought-after speaker.

Farmers came out of the fields to hear her talk about being beaten for not understanding English.

A photographic image from an 1847 daguerreotype featuring three leading abolitionists. From left, William Lloyd Garrison, publisher of The Liberator; *Wendell Phillips, known as abolition's "Golden Trumpet"; and George Thompson, a noted British abolitionist.*

They laughed and wept when they heard her personal account of hardships endured while a slave, and the indignities she had experienced as a free woman of color.

Following the name that defined her work, Sojourner wandered from place to place, speaking to all those who would listen. She moved into Connecticut and Massachusetts, eventually arriving in Northampton, a town located on the Connecticut River in Massachusetts. Her friends later described her as "a commanding figure" with a dignified manner. She "hushed every trifler into silence," where "whole audiences melted into tears by her touching stories."

She visited the Northampton Association of Education and Industry, a cooperative community where members shared equally in the operation and profit of a silkworm farm and the making of silk fabric. Sojourner was impressed with the way in which the people worked together in harmony. Sam Hill and George Benson, cofounders of the cooperative, had heard about Sojourner from friends and they asked her to stay with them. Although Hill and Benson were nothing like Pierson and Matthias, she exercised caution before getting involved too quickly.

Since The Kingdom debacle she had avoided groups that tended toward fanaticism, especially loud outbursts. When she found herself in such a group, she noted with characteristic wit: "The

Lord might come, move all through the camp, and go away again and they'd never know it because of all the noise and commotion." Then she scolded them saying, "Here you are talking about being changed in the twinkling of an eye. If the Lord should come, he'd change you to nothing, for there is nothing in you."

Sojourner stayed at Northampton in spite of her uneasiness. Northampton, a friendly haven for leading abolitionists, turned out to be a training ground for Sojourner's work as an abolitionist and feminist.

Wendell Phillips visited frequently. Sojourner learned that he was called Abolition's Golden Trumpet, because of his powerful speaking abilities. In fact, Wendell Phillips brought Samuel Hill into the movement.

Parker Pillsbury was another distinguished abolitionist who visited Northampton regularly, too. At first, Sojourner felt intimidated by the big red-bearded man whose booming voice shook the chandeliers. He had rightfully earned a reputation for being an uncompromising abolitionist who stubbornly refused to back down when the issue involved slavery. Pillsbury often spoke at meetings, wearing a torn frock coat, said to have been ripped off his back by a pro-slavery mob. "If they'd caught me, they would have ripped off my head," he said. "But I would have still gone on talking against slavers!"

Under the Fugitive Slave Act, runaways and even freedmen and women could be legally returned or forcibly removed to slave territory and sold.

David Ruggles lived in Northampton, too. Sojourner had never met him while they both lived in New York, but at Northampton they became good friends.

Although Ruggles had been born free in Norwich, Connecticut, he had worked most of his life in New York for the abolitionist movement. He donated his skills as a writer and editor of the quarterly magazine *The Mirror of Liberty* to fight the system legally. Privately he served as secretary of the underground New York Vigilance Committee, which illegally helped runaway slaves escape. He and his friend William Sill have been credited with helping to free over 600 fugitives while serving as conductors on the Underground Railroad.

Ruggles had gone blind and no doubt would have ended up living on the streets, if it hadn't been for his friends at Northampton. There he experimented with hydrotherapeutic treatment, which he credited with helping him regain partial sight. He continued his research and, in 1846, he opened a water-cure institute at Northampton. Ruggles's success as a hydrotherapist earned him the title "doctor," even though he hadn't had any formal medical training.

The children at Northampton loved the gentle activist, whose stories were as full of excitement and adventure as any written in a book, especially those about runaway slaves like his good friend Frederick Douglass.

Douglass often came to Northampton for a hot-water treatment. By that time, he had become an active member of the abolitionist movement. His reputation as a speaker was outstanding, and his voice was among those most respected. But his eloquence proved to be a disadvantage. Douglass's diction was so perfect, Southerners spread rumors that he had never been a slave. To prove he wasn't a hoax, he'd written his autobiography in 1845 giving names, dates, and events pertinent to his life. Although Sojourner couldn't read *Narrative of Frederick Douglass*, she had it read to her.

Douglass, who was still a runaway, could have

been recaptured and taken back to the South according to the Fugitive Slave Law. So he left the United States for a while, returning after his freedom had been bought by abolitionists in England.

Douglass never forgot his old friend Ruggles, and whenever he was in the area, he stopped in Northampton to visit. Often Douglass came with William Lloyd Garrison, a leading abolitionist from Massachusetts.

To some, William Lloyd Garrison was the preeminent leader of the anti-slavery movement. He was a tall, gaunt-faced man whose angry speeches were betrayed by his gentle eyes. "Prejudice against color is rebellion against God," he said.

When Belle was still living in New Paltz, Garrison, at age twenty-three, had committed his life to ending slavery. In 1832, he'd formed the New England Anti-Slavery Society, the first to call for the immediate emancipation of all slaves, and he was in Philadelphia a year later when the American Anti-Slavery Society was formed. Garrison's newspaper, *The Liberator*, inspired thousands who read it, especially his friends at Northampton. As a youth, he had even served time in prison for his beliefs. As an adult he had never wavered. The masthead of *The Liberator* expressed without reservation the sentiments of the editor: "No union with slaveholders."

Frederick Douglass was the only black representative in the Anti-Slavery Society, although other blacks were involved in other abolitionist organizations. Douglass and Garrison pushed for peaceful solutions, but other blacks disagreed. Twenty-seven-year-old Henry Highland Garnet, a Presbyterian minister, gave a rousing speech at the 1843 National Black Convention that met at Buffalo, New York. Seventy blacks attended the meeting, when Garnet called for his enslaved brothers to rise up in revolt and to hold general strikes:

> *You had better all die-die immediately —*
> *than live slaves and entail your wretchedness*
> *upon your posterity. If you would be free in*
> *this generation, here is your only hope. . . .*
> *But you are a patient people. You act as*

A picture of the convention of the Anti-Slavery Society.

Henry Highland Garnet labored as a slave blacksmith in Maryland before escaping to New York City where he was educated and served as a Presbyterian minister.

though you were made for the special use of those devils. You act as though your daughters were born to pamper the lusts of your masters and overseers. And worse than all, you tamely submit while your lords tear your wives from your embraces and defile them before your eyes. In the name of God, we ask, are you men? Where is the blood of your fathers? Has it run out of your veins? Awake! Awake! millions of voices are calling you! Your dead fathers speak to you from their graves.

Douglass answered Garnet's speech and called for moral persuasion to end slavery. Sojourner listened as the newspaper accounts were read to her.

As much as she hated slavery, she could not support violence in any form. She made a choice to stay in the Douglass-Garrison camp.

While she was at Northampton, Sojourner was also introduced to the women's equality movement.

Olive Gilbert, an early feminist and a member of the Northampton society, read Sojourner an article in *The Liberator*, reporting on the first Woman's Rights Convention in Seneca Falls, New York, July 19–20, 1848. Douglass was the only male to play a prominent role at the convention, which had been planned by two New England women, Elizabeth Cady Stanton and Lucretia Coffin Mott.

At the second session, Stanton submitted a resolution calling for women's suffrage — the right to vote! William Lloyd Garrison disapproved and even Lucretia Mott, at this time, parted with Stanton on that issue. Mott felt women's suffrage was too radical to introduce so soon; she feared it might cost the women's movement valuable support. Stanton insisted that the suffrage resolution stay in. Every resolution passed without a hitch, but with the help of Frederick Douglass — the only male in favor — the suffrage resolution passed "with a narrow margin."

Gilbert, who had become Sojourner's reading partner, shared an article in Douglass's newspaper, *The North Star*, that summarized the convention from his point of view: "We are free to say that in respect to political rights, we hold woman to be justly entitled to all we claim for man."

Once again Sojourner listened to all the articles and conversations around her. Nineteenth-century women had very few political rights. True. But free black women had fewer still. A slave woman was brutally mistreated by white men and women, and very often by black men, who modeled their behavior after their masters.

Lydia Marie Child, an author and abolitionist, who, with her husband, published The National Anti-Slavery Standard, *a New York weekly newspaper.*

* * *

Lydia Marie Child was a nineteenth-century female humanist and author. As a humanist she supported a philosophy that believed in the dignity and worth of humankind. Child described the appalling social status of the slave woman:

[She is] *unprotected either by law or public opinion. She is the property of her master, and her daughters are his property . . . they must be entirely subservient to the will of their owner on pain of being whipped as near to death as will comport with his interest or quite to death if it suits his pleasure.*

White women were part of the same zoo, but in a little larger cage. They were controlled by the men in their lives — fathers, brothers, uncles — who trained them to believe they were too "fragile" to make social or political decisions. Charles Dickens observed during his visit to the states that "American men accorded their women more deference, lavished more money on them, regarded them with more respect than was accorded the women of any country. But they didn't particularly like them."

Women, though not slaves, couldn't hold public office, serve on juries, or even manage their own money — if they had any. In the event of a divorce, the husband was given custody of the

SOJOURNER TRUTH.

The frontispiece from Sojourner Truth's narrative.

children, because as one judge summed it up, "If she had been a good wife and mother, sharp on her duties, then her husband wouldn't be seeking separation."

But more importantly, without the right to vote, women remained powerless to change their condition.

When Sojourner listened and observed the struggle of women — black and white — she decided that women's rights, too, was a cause worth fighting for.

Frederick Douglass had written his autobiography. So, Olive Gilbert encouraged Sojourner to write her own story, and even offered to write it as Sojourner dictated it. Garrison immediately saw the advantage of adding Sojourner's story to the growing collection of anti-slavery literature. Her story was unique because it revealed how slaves in the North had been treated. He offered to print it and even wrote the introduction to *Narrative of Sojourner Truth: A Northern Slave*.

The book was published in 1850, the same year Congress passed a more rigid version of the Fugitive Slave Act in the Compromise of 1850. In retrospect it is easy to chart the events that led up to the Civil War from this point. The Compromise of 1850 was a key issue that fanned the smoldering coals of discontent in the North and the South.

After the Mexican War, Representative David

Wilmot of Pennsylvania introduced an amendment to a pending bill in Congress, which sought to prohibit slavery in any territory acquired as a result of the Mexican War, that is, the Southwest territory. The amendment passed the House, but was defeated in the Senate. Bitter debates followed, with fistfights almost breaking out on the Senate floor. If New Mexico and California were admitted as free states, that would upset the balance of Southern and Northern senators that stood at 15–15.

In September 1850, Congress enacted the infamous compromise. California was admitted as a free state in exchange for the passage of a new and tougher fugitive slave law to replace the poorly enforced act of 1793. The compromise settled nothing. Abolitionists were determined to fight the expansion of slavery into the West, and Southerners hid behind states' rights to defend slavery.

Meanwhile, the Northampton Association closed. The silkworm business wasn't very profitable. At least the idea had worked, so Sojourner wasn't too disappointed. George Benson bought the factory building and Sam Hill took the silk. Hill offered to build Sojourner a house so she'd have some security in her advancing years. Sojourner promised to pay him back the $300 it cost, which she would earn from the sale of her book.

Chapter 7
Ain't I a Woman?

The Fugitive Slave Act of 1793 gave slaveholders, or their agents, the right to capture runaways and return them to their masters. Persons who were caught helping a runaway could be fined $500. For the most part the act had been ignored by abolitionists, and between 1830 and 1850 they had helped close to fifty thousand slaves escape through the Underground Railroad.

Southerners and pro-slavery sympathizers pushed for and passed the stronger Fugitive Slave Act of 1850. It only served to increase mounting hostilities between the North and South. Slave owners argued that enforcement of the act protected their property rights. Northerners argued that the law encouraged professional slave catchers to kidnap free people of color and take them to the South.

Many people who weren't abolitionists didn't agree with the Fugitive Slave Act. There was something distasteful about recapturing people who had gone through so much to free themselves. Hadn't the United States been founded by people freeing themselves of tyranny?

While abolitionists continued in their battle to end slavery, slaves also worked to emancipate themselves. One of the principal characters in the struggle for freedom was Harriet Tubman, a fugitive slave and conductor on the Underground Railroad.

Sojourner didn't met Tubman until many years later, but she knew about and admired the woman's bold spirit and determination.

Tubman had escaped from slavery in 1849, but she had returned to the South to lead others to freedom. For her work as a conductor on the Underground Railroad, Harriet had a price on her head. It didn't matter to her; she was committed to eventually making twenty trips back to the South to lead hundreds of slaves to freedom.

Abolitionists took delight in telling stories about Tubman and other daring escapes. None thrilled the audiences more than the account of William and Ellen Craft. In 1847, Ellen, a fairskinned black, posed as a white man traveling with her slave, who was in fact, her husband. In this way the Crafts escaped from Georgia and made a mockery of the entire social system based on color inferiority. Why, whites couldn't tell who was one of their own!

*William and Ellen Craft escaped to freedom when Ellen Craft
dressed up in the clothes of a male planter and her
husband traveled as her servant.*

Sojourner watched events like these unfolding
around her, and she often expressed her joy at
being "near" those who were so passionate about
freeing her people. Her book hadn't sold too well
because she didn't have the national recognition
Douglass and some other abolitionists had. So,
Sojourner went to abolitionist gatherings and sold
her book afterward.

At a meeting one evening in late 1850, Garrison
saw his friend Sojourner in the audience. He said
matter-of-factly, "Sojourner will say a few words,
after which Wendell Phillips will follow."

Sojourner hadn't come prepared to speak, but
she didn't pass up the opportunity, either. When
she stood up, her presence commanded attention.

Then, just as she had done at the camp meetings, she used the strength of her voice to capture her audience.

She began with one of her "home-made" hymns:

> I am pleading for my people,
> A poor downtrodden race,
> Who dwell in freedom's boasted land,
> With no abiding place.
>
> I am pleading that my people
> May have their rights restored;
> For they have long been toiling,
> And yet have no reward.
>
> They are forced the crops to culture,
> But not for them they yield,
> Although both late and early
> They labor in the field.
>
> Whilst I bear upon my body
> the scars of many a gash,
> I am pleading for my people
> Who groan beneath the lash.

Then, without fanfare, she began her speech, making point after point with eloquent simplicity. "Well, Children," she began, "I was born a slave in Ulster County, New York. I don't know if it was summer or winter, fall or spring. I don't even know what day of the week it was. They don't care when a slave is born or when he dies . . . just how much work they can do."

After finishing the tragic story of her father's death and how she'd fought to get Peter back, she closed: "God will not make his face to shine upon a nation that holds with slavery." The crowd cheered and applauded. Some people sobbed while others sat stunned and silent. It was a hard act even for Wendell Phillips to follow.

Sojourner sold twice as many books that evening. So, she decided to go on a speaking tour . . . to sell books and to spread the "truth" as she understood it. People also wanted to know about the hymns. So, she made up some, had them printed, and sold them along with her biography. Sojourner dutifully put aside money to pay for the printing of her book and to pay Sam Hill for building her house.

Sojourner accepted an invitation to speak at the first national Woman's Rights Convention in Worchester, Massachusetts.

The clergy took an active role in resisting the women's meeting. One minister promised to expel women in his congregation who attended the meeting, while another clergyman proclaimed it a "meeting sponsored by the devil."

The male-dominated press didn't make it any better. Reporters and essayists called the conference a hen party and chided the women, saying

A plaque in Seneca Falls, New York, honoring the first Women's Rights Convention in 1848. It states, "Elizabeth Cady Stanton moved this resolution: 'That it is the duty of the women of this country to secure to themselves their sacred right to the elective franchise.' "

they were "hens that wanted to crow," and "fe-he-males."

Yet one thousand participants from eleven states showed up on that late October day in 1850. Sojourner found it interesting that several men had come to support the women; among them Douglass, Garrison, Pillsbury, and Phillips; but she noticed right away that she was the only black female present.

Harriot Hunt, a self-educated physician, officially opened the meeting by reading a statement from Mrs. Elizabeth Cady Stanton, who regrettably couldn't be there because she was at home in Seneca Falls, New York, awaiting the birth of her fourth child. The chairwoman then gave a powerful speech that ended with, "We claim for women all the blessings which the other sex has, solely, or by her aid, achieved for itself."

Sojourner tried to be patient while speaker after speaker raised questions such as whether women should be able to keep their jewelry after a divorce or whether women were more liberated by wearing bloomers, a pant-type dress, which supposedly freed the body and allowed more physical exercise. Both issues seemed irrelevant to Sojourner. She was more concerned about whether a mother should be allowed to keep her children after a divorce. And the whole idea of bloomers amused her. She'd worn pantlike dresses over a washtub many a day, so the style held no glamour for her.

Then Lucretia Mott, the young schoolteacher, spoke passionately about being paid less than a male teacher simply because she was a woman. Lucy Stone, a graduate of Oberlin College, was equally concerned. She told the group that she had refused to use her husband's last name to show he was not her "master." Equal pay for equal work and personal self-worth — these were issues with which Sojourner could identify. Her interest increased.

During the speeches, Sojourner made mental notes. When it was her turn to speak she said: "Sisters, I'm not clear what you be after. If women want any rights more than they've got, why don't they just take them and not be talking about it."

The conference goals might have been fuzzy at first, but by the end of the conference there was no doubt about what the women wanted. Their motto clearly stated their primary objective: "Equality before the law without distinction of sex or color." And on this they all agreed, especially Sojourner, who left the conference feeling inspired and motivated. From that time on, Sojourner included equality for women in her speeches.

For a while, Sojourner traveled and spoke with Garrison and George Thompson, an English abolitionist. Often they reached places where their figures had just been burned in effigy. Her speeches always managed to stir the emotions of a sympathetic gathering or inflame the tempers of a hostile group. No one could listen to Sojourner passively.

After a fall filled with travel and speeches she was tired and due for a rest. She stayed the winter with Amy and Isaac Post, well-known Quaker abolitionists, in Rochester, New York. Letters from her children finally caught up with her there.

Elizabeth, Hannah, and Diana had married and had started families of their own. Sojourner longed to see them. Diana wrote that Dumont had "gone West" with some of his sons, but before leaving he had become a strong abolitionist, saying "slavery was an evil institution."

Sojourner wasn't surprised, because the last time she'd seen her old master his attitude had begun

Amy Post, a Quaker along with her husband, Isaac, were prominent members of the abolitionist cause in the Rochester, New York, area.

to change. In an updated version of her autobiography, Sojourner recalled what Dumont had said:

Now the sin of slavery is so clearly written out, and so much talked against, — why the whole world cries out against it! — that if any one says he don't know, and has not heard, he must, I think, be a liar. In my slaveholding days, there were few that spoke against it, and these few made little impression on anyone. Had it been as it is now, think you I could have held slaves? No! I should not have dared to do it, but should have emancipated every one of them.

Although the Posts begged her to stay, Sojourner wanted to move on. She heard about an anti-slavery convention to be held in Ohio, so Sojourner felt God was telling her to go West. As always she obeyed.

In 1851 Ohio was a free state and a main artery on the Underground Railroad, but there was a lot of pro-slavery sentiment there, especially in rural areas. Pro-slavery Northerners were called *Copperheads*.

Sojourner's audiences changed drastically. Sometimes she was well-received, but more often than not she ended up hoarse from having to yell over protestors' hoots and jeers. One day she was met outside of a town by an angry mob led by

*Fugitives traveled in groups to safety
in the Northern states and Canada.*

Copperheads and told to go someplace else. Sojourner walked away but circled around and came into town from another direction. On another occasion a sheriff arrested Sojourner and her companion to keep them from being hurt. Giving up was out of the question, however, even though her work had become dangerous.

Sojourner was lecturing in Ohio when someone told her there was going to be a Woman's Rights Convention in Akron, Ohio, organized by Mrs. Frances Gage. Sojourner decided to attend.

Hundreds of men and women gathered at a local church to hear what the various speakers had to say. Clearly the audience was of mixed opinions

on the subject of women's rights. Most of the men
had come with unyielding prejudices, clergymen
mostly who tried to discredit the women's movement as anti-Christian. A few women had come
accompanied by their enlightened husbands or
male companions. Some women came alone, but
with their husband's or father's "permission."
Then there were the seasoned feminists who came
because, at last, their goals and aspirations were
being addressed.

The gathering was large but for the most part
congenial. Suddenly, the doors swung open and a
tall, proud figure stood framed in the doorway.
"It's Sojourner Truth," someone whispered.
Slowly Sojourner walked to the front of the
church, noticing she was the only black person
there. Since there were no seats left, she took a
seat on the steps to the pulpit. She folded her arms
and listened.

Soon the room was buzzing. Was a black woman
going to speak?

One speaker after another came to the podium,
each trying to impress his or her opinion upon the
crowd. Several preachers tried to disrupt the meeting by encouraging women "who feared God" to
leave immediately. When that didn't work, the
preachers used the same tired logic that had been
used for centuries to oppress women and blacks.
*God created women to be weak and blacks to be a
subservient race.*

One clergyman argued that Jesus was a man and that if God had intended women to be equal He "would have at that time made some gesture to show his intent."

Another man quoted a newspaper article which suggested that "a woman's place is at home taking care of her children." (*What?* thought Sojourner. *Nobody ever gave me that opportunity.*)

Then, of course, there was the persistent argument that woman had sinned first and therefore revealed her inferiority.

During a brief intermission, a group of women cornered Frances Gage and questioned whether Sojourner would be allowed to speak. They were afraid that having a black woman speak might confuse the issues and even discredit their cause. After all, *what has women's rights to do with abolition?* Some of the "leading" ladies were threatening to leave.

"Let's just see," Mrs. Gage answered, making no commitment either way.

When the next session began, Sojourner approached the pulpit. "No, no, don't let her speak," several men and women called out.

Sojourner turned to the chairwoman asking for permission. Gage hesitated momentarily, then simply introduced her, "Sojourner Truth." That's all that was needed.

By then Sojourner was used to facing hostile crowds. Fearlessly, but gently, she took control of the situation. First, she removed her sunbonnet, folded it neatly and set it aside. Her slow deliberate movements had a calming affect on the audience.

All morning she'd listened to preachers — men who ought to know better — use the Bible to support their own dead-end purposes. She was furious and ready to do battle using God's own truth. With no prepared speech in front of her she began in a deep, husky voice:

"Well, Children, where there is so much racket, there must be somethin' out of kilter. . . . The white men will be in a fix pretty soon. But what's all this about anyway?

"That man over there," she said pointing to a minister who had said a woman's place was to be mother, wife and companion, good sister, and loving niece. Among other things he also said women were the "weaker sex."

To this Sojourner took issue. "He says women need to be helped into carriages and lifted over ditches and to have the best everywhere. Nobody ever helps me into carriages, over mud puddles, or gets me any best places."

And raising herself to her full height, she asked, "And ain't I a woman?"

Sojourner turned to the men who were seated behind her. "Look at me!" She bared her right arm and raised it in the air. The audience gasped as one voice. Her dark arm was muscular, made strong by hard work. "I have ploughed. And I have

"I Sell the Shadow to Support the Substance." Truth
distributed leaflets with this phrase to support the
abolitionist cause.

planted." No doubt she was remembering the year
she had worked for Dumont to earn early freedom.
"And I have gathered into barns. And no man
could head me." She paused again and asked this
time in a whisper. "And ain't I a woman?"

"I have borne [thirteen] children and seen them
sold into slavery, and when I cried out in a mother's grief, none heard me but Jesus. And ain't I a
woman?" (No doubt Sojourner was thinking about
her mother but used "I" instead. Sojourner only
had five children.)

Then one by one she took on the male religious
pedants. "You say Jesus was a man so that means
God favors men over women. Where did your
Christ come from?" She asked again. "Where did
he come from?" Then she answered her own question. "From God and a woman. Man had nothing
to do with him."

She challenged the widely held belief that
women were less intelligent than men, and blacks
had no intellect at all. "Suppose a man's mind
holds a quart, and woman's don't hold but a pint;
if her pint is full, it's as good as a quart." Her
common sense ripped at the core of male hypoc-
risy.

Sojourner directed her conclusion to the women
in the audience. "If the first woman God ever made
was strong enough to turn the world upside down
all alone, these women together ought to be able

to turn it back and get it right-side up again and now that they are asking to do it, the men better let 'em."

Few listeners at the time could understand the full import of what Sojourner Truth was really saying in that hard-hitting "Ain't I a Woman?" speech. It is doubtful the rural farm community was ready to accept the claim that took women's rights across the boundaries of race, class, and the bondage of slavery.

Sojourner's "truth" was simple. Racism and sexism were unacceptable to people of good reason.

Chapter 8
Keep 'Em Scratchin'

Sojourner left Akron with a banner her friends had made stating: "Proclaim liberty throughout all the land unto all the inhabitants thereof." Loaded with 600 copies of her book, she traveled around Ohio and Indiana in a borrowed horse and buggy, making speeches against slavery and for women's rights. She never worried about food, clothing, or shelter, and often let her horse choose the direction she would go. "The Lord will guide and protect me," she said with absolute faith.

The Fugitive Slave Law continued to be a thorn in the side of abolitionists. At the Anniversary Convention of the Anti-Slavery Society in Salem, Ohio, Frederick Douglass expressed his belief that war was the only way freedom would ever be won. Douglass's long-standing nonviolent position changed and caused a strain between himself and Garrison. He said, nevertheless, "There is no longer any hope for justice other than bloody rebellion. Slavery must end in blood."

Sojourner was in the audience. *There is no hope . . . There is no hope!* The words struck at her heart like a hot knife. She leaped to her feet. "Frederick," she called out to her old friend in a voice that trembled with emotion. "Frederick, is God dead?"

Recognizing his friend, Frederick understood her meaning. He also knew that Sojourner was asking if he had lost his faith. "No," he answered quickly. "And because God is not dead, slavery can only end in blood."

But Sojourner wasn't willing to accept that outlook. She clung to the idea that slavery could end without violence.

Sojourner's fame and stature as an abolitionist and feminist with wit and wisdom spread across the Midwestern countryside. Even her opponents had to respect her.

Once a heckler in an Ohio town shouted out that the Constitution didn't say a word against slavery. "Are you against the Constitution, old woman?"

"Well, Children," Sojourner began in her usual way, "I talks to God and God talks to me. This morning I was walking out and I climbed over a fence. I saw the wheat holdin' up its head, lookin' so big. I goes up and take hold of it. Would you believe it, there was no wheat there! I says, 'God, what's the matter with this wheat?' And He says to me, 'Sojourner, there's a little weevil in it.' "

"What's that got to do with the Constitution?" the heckler yelled back.

Sojourner held up her hand to let them know she wasn't finished. "I hears talk about the Constitution and the rights of man. I comes up and I takes hold of this Constitution. It looks mighty big. And I feels for my rights. But they not there. Then I says, 'God, what ails this Constitution?' And you know what He says to me? God says, 'Sojourner, there's a little weevil in it.' " This was something the Ohio farmers of 1852 could understand, because their wheat crop had been ruined by a tiny beetle called a weevil.

There was an antislavery meeting in Ashtabula County, Ohio, and Sojourner was there along with her good friend, Parker Pillsbury, who was the primary speaker. Pillsbury gave an eloquent and moving speech against slavery, after which a young lawyer spoke for almost an hour about the inferiority of blacks. He said blacks were "fit only for slavery. As a race, the Negro is only a connecting link between man and animals."

Meanwhile a terrible storm approached. The wind, thunder, and lightning raged outside the small church. Trees were uprooted and rain fell in a blinding sheet.

The lawyer called out that it was God's wrath, come to show He was angry with the anti-slavery movement. But Sojourner stepped out of the darkness. Dressed in the familiar white turban, gray dress, and shawl, she approached the stage.

"You afraid the Lord has sent the storm in wrath at our opinions?" she asked the lawyer, leaning over as if to comfort a little boy. "Child," she said, "don't be scared. You're not goin' to be harmed. Why, I don't s'pect God's even heard about you yet."

Once a man asked, "Do you think your talk about slavery does any good? Do you suppose people care what you say? Why I don't care any more for your talk than I do for the bite of a flea."

Sojourner laughed. "Lord willing I'll keep you scratchin'."

Southerners felt pressed to defend their way of life against the onslaught of criticism hurled at them by Northern "meddlers." George Fitzhugh, a Virginia slaveholder, wrote in 1854 that blacks were better off slaves in America than "a far more cruel slavery in Africa, or from idolatry and cannibalism, and every brutal crime that can disgrace humanity."

Fitzhugh was often quoted by anti-slavery speakers. Sojourner was alert and ready with an answer for those who did use Fitzhugh's erroneous material: "Be careful," she'd say forcefully, "God will not stand with wrong; never mind how right you think you be."

Politically, the country was divided North

against South, but what about territories in the West? Many thought the expansion of slavery into western parts of the country had been regulated by the Missouri Compromise of 1820. At that time, Missouri was admitted as a slave state while at the same time Maine was admitted as a free state. Since the senate seats remained balanced, it was acceptable to both sides that slavery would be outlawed in lands within the Louisiana Purchase north of the parallel 36 30′.

But tensions between pro- and anti-slavery forces continued to mount; everybody knew something had to be done. The Kansas-Nebraska bill was introduced in the senate by Senator Stephen A. Douglas from Illinois. It passed in May, 1854,

Senator Charles Sumner of Massachusetts sharply criticized the role of the South during the debates on the Kansas-Nebraska Act.

John Brown was considered a radical abolitionist. Along with members of his family, Brown joined forces with the Free State Party to secure Kansas as a "free" territory.

giving citizens living in a territory seeking statehood the right to choose whether they wanted to be a slave state or a free state. Contrary to what the supporters of the act had hoped, it didn't solve a thing. The Kansas Territory located west of Missouri, a slave state, became a political hotbed.

Border ruffians from Missouri crossed over into Kansas to vote for Kansas to be admitted as a slave state. Free-Soil Kansas residents rejected the vote and refused to accept the provisional slave-state government. Armed conflict was inevitable.

In May 1856, pro-slavery forces attacked Lawrence, a Free-Soil settlement. John Brown, a radical abolitionist, had gone to Kansas to push for its entrance as a free state. After the destruction

of Lawrence, Brown led a counterattack against a
pro-slavery settlement in Pottawatomie Creek.
Five settlers were killed. The incident became so
heated that Preston S. Brooks, a congressman from
South Carolina, physically attacked Massachusetts
Senator Charles Sumner on the senate floor after
Sumner finished making an anti-slavery speech.
Sumner was beaten so badly he was an invalid for
over three years.

Brooks gave Sojourner and other abolitionists
plenty of ammunition with which to show Southern cruelty and disregard for human rights. Southerners, on the other hand, used John Brown to
illustrate abolitionists' extremism.

From 1851 to 1857, Sojourner "kept 'em
scratchin' " in Ohio and Indiana. Sometime in
late summer of 1853, she'd gone back East. But
before going to her house in Northampton, Massachusetts, Sojourner stopped to visit with Harriet
Beecher Stowe, the author of *Uncle Tom's Cabin,
or Life Among the Lowly*.

The daughter of Lyman Beecher and the wife
of Charles Ellis Stowe (both Calvanist clergymen
and abolitionists), Harriet had written the novel
in 1852 as a response to the Fugitive Slave Act.
By 1856, over two million copies had been sold.
One reviewer said the book "penetrated the walls
of Congress and made the politicians tremble. It
startled statesmen, who scented danger near."

Sojourner had had the book read to her as soon as a copy was made available. The story is about Tom, a slave who saves his master's daughter and is promised his freedom. But his master dies before Tom is actually freed. The family falls upon hard times and Tom is sold to a horrible slaveowner named Simon Legree. Legree tried everything to degrade Tom, but Tom holds firmly to his religious convictions. In a frenzy of anger, Legree beats Tom to death.

The two women liked each other immediately and respected the work each was doing to end slavery. Sojourner spoke to a gathering at Mrs. Stowe's home.

Stowe later wrote: "No princess could have received a drawing-room with more composed dignity than Sojourner her audience. She stood among them, calm, erect, as one of her own native palm trees waving alone in the desert."

Now Sojourner was sixty years old. It was time to retire and enjoy the life she'd dreamed of for years. So, in 1857, she sold her Northampton house for $750 and moved to Harmonia, Michigan, a short distance from Battle Creek.

By 1860, her daughter Elizabeth Banks moved there with her son Sammy. They were also joined by Diana and her husband, Jacob Corbin, who was a hotel clerk. They had one son, Frank. (Sophia's son, William Boyd, was the same age as Frank.)

In 1857, there were fifty-four other blacks in
Battle Creek, and the mayor was a conductor on
the Underground Railroad. The townspeople were
honored to have such a famous person living
among them. They helped Sojourner convert an
old barn on College Street into a comfortable
house, and there she planned to spend her last
days, enjoying her grandchildren.

From the start, Sammy Banks, Elizabeth's son
by her second marriage, favored his grandmother.
He begged to stay with her, and she welcomed his
companionship. When he was young, he ran errands and did chores for his grandmother and,
when he learned to read, Sammy read the Bible
to her. In many ways Sammy became Sojourner's
substitute for her lost son, Peter.

For a while, Sojourner was content to sit on the
front porch, telling stories, singing hymns, and
smoking a white clay pipe. Once she had been
criticized for smoking a pipe, a habit she picked
up when she was a child, working for the Schryvers
back in New Paltz. "The Bible tells us that no
unclean thing can enter the Kingdom of Heaven."

Sojourner responded, "True, but when I go to
Heaven I expect to leave my breath behind me."

In 1857 the Supreme Court added still another
wedge in the ever-widening gulf between North
and South. Dred Scott, a slave, had sued for his
freedom because he had lived in a free state. The
court ruled that a slave was "property," and there-

fore not a citizen. Scott didn't have the right to sue. The decision was a blow to abolitionists, but it didn't really affect Scott. His "owner" freed him immediately after the case was final.

Sojourner felt that this was no time to retreat. Against her daughter's wishes, she planned another speaking tour. Before leaving, she had her autobiography updated. Frances Titus, a friend and neighbor who helped Sojourner with her correspondence, would edit and expand the *Narrative* six times between 1853 and 1884. Sojourner also designed a postcard with her photograph on it. At the bottom was her message: "I sell the shadow to support the substance." She sold it along with her book and hymns. Then, taking Sammy with her, Sojourner went back out on the speaking tour at age sixty-two.

After a year, Frances Titus volunteered to become her traveling companion and "manager." And together the two women spoke to anti-slavery groups. "Slavery must be destroyed, root and branch," Sojourner told audiences.

Indiana was a difficult place for an abolitionist. While speaking in Kosciusko County with her good friend, Parker Pillsbury, Sojourner experienced a vicious personal attack. A pro-slavery group, led by a local doctor, claimed Sojourner wasn't a woman, insisting that she was a man impersonating a woman.

"We demand," said the leader, "if it be a she,

Frances Walling Titus, a dear friend and traveling companion of Sojourner Truth.

that she expose her breast to the gaze of some of the ladies present so that they may report back and dispel the audience's doubts."

Pillsbury leaped to Sojourner's defense, but she stopped him. "Why do you suppose me to be a man?"

The doctor based his claim on her voice that he said "is not the voice of a woman." After a moment of hesitation Sojourner slowly unbuttoned her blouse. "I will show my breast," she said to everyone's astonishment, "but to the entire congregation. It is not my shame but yours that I do this."

At another time, when told they were going to burn down the meeting hall where she was scheduled to speak, Sojourner replied, "I'll speak on the ashes."

There were times when Sojourner did more than just speak to large audiences. Olive Gilbert wrote in her own journal an incident that happened while they traveled together.

> There was at the time an invalid in the house, and Sojourner, on learning it, felt a mission to go and comfort her. It was curious to see the tall, gaunt, dusky figure stalk up to the bed with such an air of conscious authority, and take on herself the office of consoler with such a mixture of authority and tenderness.

Sojourner was older. Olive noticed that it was

harder for her to get started in the morning: "But
once she is up, she can go as long as a woman half
her age." Another observer noticed that though
Sojourner had aged, "There was both power and
sweetness in that great warm soul and that vigorous
frame." She was still able to "keep 'em scratchin'."

Chapter 9
The Book of Life

There were at least two hundred slave uprisings between 1800 and 1859, led by bold black leaders. Three come to mind immediately: Gabriel Prosser, Denmark Vesey, and Nat Turner.

The mere mention of their names struck fear in the hearts of slaveholders. In 1800, Prosser had organized and armed slaves who were prepared to take Richmond, Virginia, by force, but he had been betrayed and hanged before he could carry out his plan. In 1822, Vesey, a free black man, recruited nine thousand slaves to take part in an attack on Charleston, South Carolina. He, too, was betrayed and hanged along with hundreds of his followers. Then, in 1831, Turner, a Virginia slave, led an insurrection that resulted in the death of sixty whites. The authorities captured and hanged him, too.

Southerners knew that blacks outnumbered them 3–1, so they had reason to worry about re-

bellions. A female relative of George Washington
put it succinctly: "We know that death in the most
horrid form threatens us." This fear may be partly
the reason why slaves received swift and severe
punishment for *any* form of disloyalty to the
master.

Sojourner argued that slave masters had much
more to fear than slave insurrections. "It is God
the slave owner will answer to on the day of
judgment."

Prosser, Vesey, and Turner caused a rip in the
fabric of American politics. But, John Brown's
1859 raid on Harpers Ferry, Virginia (now West
Virginia), ripped it in two. Since the Kansas border wars, Brown had become a radical who advocated an armed attack against the South to free
the slaves and train them as soldiers to free other
slaves. He often said slaveholders had "forfeited
their right to live."

Brown's plan was to capture arms at the military
arsenal at Harpers Ferry, then free slaves through
force. The plan failed, and Brown was captured
and hanged on December 2, 1859.

Although Sojourner Truth was illiterate, she
stayed well-informed, especially about political affairs. Sammy read her every detail about Brown's
trial and execution. Southerners accused Brown
of being a maniacal murderer. And, at first, more
than a few moderate abolitionists tried to distance

themselves from Brown's firebrand methods —
but the grass-roots support for him was overwhelm-
ing. So, although Brown only represented a small
faction in the movement during his life, *all* abolitionists embraced him in death. Brown became
a martyred folk hero, a symbol of freedom.

Everywhere people were singing "John Brown's
Body." It was very popular. Later during the Civil
War, Julia Ward Howe wrote "The Battle Hymn
of the Republic" to the music of "John Brown's
Body." It was a personal favorite of Abraham
Lincoln.

Sammy also kept Sojourner informed about the
upcoming presidential election. She was particularly interested in Abraham Lincoln and the new
Republican Party. She instructed Sammy to read
her articles about Lincoln whenever he found
them.

Sojourner liked what she knew about candidate
Lincoln. He had made himself quite clear on the
slavery issue during a debate with Senator Douglas
in 1858:

*A house divided against itself cannot stand! I
believe this government cannot endure perma-
nently half slave and half free. I do not expect the
union to be dissolved; I do not expect the house
to fall; but I do expect it will cease to be divided.
It will become all one thing, or all the other.*

WILLIAM H. LEEMAN

JOHN E. COOK

JOHN H. COPELAND

AARON D. STEVENS

ALBERT HAZLETT

BARCLAY COPPOC

JEREMIAH ANDERSON

DAINGERFIELD NEWBY

LEWIS LEARY

*Pictured on these pages are some of the men who followed
John Brown in the famous raid at Harpers Ferry.*

OLIVER BROWN

OWEN BROWN

WATSON BROWN

DAUPHIN THOMPSON

EDWIN COPPOC

SHIELDS GREEN

STEWART TAYLOR

CHARLES P. TIDD

OSBORN ANDERSON

While Lincoln was a congressman, he had introduced a bill providing for the gradual emancipation of slaves in Washington, D.C. He opposed the opening of territories to slavery, and he had spoken out against the Dred Scott Decision. Sojourner was convinced he would be a good president, but waited to endorse him.

Most abolitionists were being cautious about Lincoln because he hadn't called for the immediate elimination of slavery. But the South so feared him that they promised to secede if he won. Lincoln was elected president in 1860. By the time he took office on March 4, 1861, seven Southern states had seceded from the union, led by South Carolina.

Sojourner was in Michigan when she got the word that a rebel general had fired on Fort Sumter and the Civil War had begun. She hadn't wanted a war, but once it started, she gave her full support to the union soldiers. She, like Frederick Douglass, was concerned that blacks weren't given an opportunity to fight for freedom, too.

Many blacks had volunteered for the service right after Sumter, but they'd been turned away. As the war progressed, Lincoln was bombarded with requests from black and white leaders to raise a "colored unit," and to allow them to serve in more ways than cooks and laborers.

In the fall of 1862, Lincoln finally yielded to the pressure and ordered an all-black unit to be established, but with white officers. The 54th Massachusetts Volunteer Infantry was a "test" of black soldiers' ability in combat. Would they run under fire? Would they follow officers? Could they be disciplined? The men of the 54th proved they could be good combat soldiers.

African-Americans' response to the 54th was phenomenal. Young blacks from all over the country went to Boston and signed up. Two of Douglass's sons joined, and Sojourner's grandson, James Caldwell, who was nineteen did, too. She said her only regret was that she couldn't take up arms herself. James, she said, had "gone forth to redeem the white people from the curse that God has sent upon them . . . I'd be on hand as the Joan of Arc, to lead the army of the Lord, for now is the day and the hour for the colored man to save his nation."

Abolitionists still weren't happy with Lincoln's reluctance to emancipate the slaves. But Sojourner gave Lincoln her support. "Children," she said, "have patience! It takes a great while to turn about this great ship of State." But abolitionists continued to pressure Lincoln.

One October day in 1862, Josephine Griffing, a feminist and abolitionist friend of Sojourner's, came to visit her in Michigan. Josephine and Sojourner had traveled throughout Ohio, sharing hardships and triumphs for the good part of a year.

"I've come," she said, "to beg your help. As

CHARLES R. DOUGLASS.

Charles and Lewis Douglass,
Frederick Douglass's two sons,
served in the celebrated
Massachusetts 54th Regiment.

you know, the president has promised to free the slaves the first of the year. The war effort is not going well . . . anti-slavery speakers are needed more than ever before to rally people to our cause. I have been asked to go into Indiana, and I want you to come with me."

Sojourner smiled. "Let me get my hat."

For the rest of 1862, Josephine and Sojourner traveled together urging people to push for the end of slavery. Josephine wrote an article for the *National Anti-Slavery Standard* in New York: "Our meetings are largely attended by persons from every part of the country . . . Slavery made a conquest in this country by the suppression of free speech, and freedom must make her conquest by the steadfast support of free speech. There are a hundred men now who would spill their blood sooner than surrender the rights of Sojourner."

Then on January 1, 1863, President Abraham Lincoln finally signed an executive order ending slavery in the rebel states.

All person held as slaves within any state or designated part of a state, the people whereof shall then be in rebellion against the United States, shall be then, thenceforward and forever free.

The Emancipation Proclamation was received in the North with cheers and tears. Church bells rang in thousands of churches. There was dancing in the streets. Sojourner gathered with her friends in Battle Creek and celebrated with singing, cheering, and long speeches. No Pinxter festival could compare to the joy and enthusiasm shared among those who had dedicated their lives to freedom.

A few days after emancipation, Sojourner Truth had a stroke. Somehow a rumor spread that she had died. Oliver Johnson, editor of the *Anti-Slavery Standard*, believing the rumor to be true, printed the story of her death. When Harriet Beecher Stowe read it she wrote an article about Sojourner, praising her life accomplishments, which was published in the *Atlantic Magazine*. Stowe titled her article "The Libyan [African] Sibyl," a name Sojourner was thereafter called.

But the great lady wasn't dead. Sojourner recovered quickly with the help of friends and family. Imagine Harriet Stowe's surprise when she received a thank-you letter from Sojourner!

It was difficult for a woman who had been busy all her life to sit still. Besides, it was no time for a seasoned abolitionist to quit. Sojourner plunged back into her work, even though her daughters begged her to at least slow down. "There's a war going on," she said. "And I mean to be a part of it."

After emancipation, fifteen hundred black troops enlisted in the 1st Michigan Volunteer Infantry. Black soldiers weren't paid the same as whites, and sometimes their white officers mistreated them. Sojourner spoke out against this kind of injustice, pointing out that, if black soldiers were dying equally, why weren't they paid equally for living?

By Thanksgiving holiday 1863, Sojourner was informed that her grandson, James Caldwell, was missing in action. He had not been seen since the morning of July 16, 1863, when the 54th saw action on James Island. Two days later the regiment had attacked Fort Wagner, South Carolina. Sammy had read the details of the battle to Sojourner in the *Standard*: "The Charleston papers all say that six hundred and fifty of our killed were buried on the Sunday morning after the assault. . . . Unofficial reports say the Negroes have been sold into slavery and that white officers are treated with unmeasured abuse."

What of James? Sojourner wondered. Was he lying in a common grave with others or was he suffering a fate worse than death — slavery?

Sojourner visited Camp Ward in Detroit, to help lift the soldiers' spirits as well as her own. She'd gone among her neighbors gathering donations of food and clothing so that the soldiers could have a good holiday.

One man said she was foolish for trying to help. Sojourner asked who he was. He answered, "I am the only son of my mother." To which Sojourner quipped: "I am glad there are no more!"

After passing out the food and clothing, she sang a song she'd composed especially for the

Sgt. William J. Carney fought with the Massachusetts
54th Regiment. He was the first of twenty-three blacks
to win the Congressional Medal of Honor. He waited
thirty-seven years for the award.

Michigan Infantry. (Sung to the tune of "John Brown's Body.")

We are the hardy soldiers of the First of Michigan;
We're fighting for the union and for the rights of man.
And when the battle wages you'll find us in the van,
As we go marching on.

We are the valiant soldiers who 'listed for the war;
We are fighting for the Union, we are fighting for the law.
We can shoot a rebel farther than a white man ever saw,
As we go marching on.

They will have to pay us wages, the wages of their sin;
They will have to bow their foreheads to their colored kith and kin;
They will have to give us house-room, or the roof will tumble in,
As we go marching on.

As the bespectacled elderly woman moved among the soldiers, serving them a "proper Thanksgiving dinner," she talked with them about their parents and home. "Can you write, son?" she asked. If the answer was yes she asked, "Have you sent your folks word of your whereabouts?" If he hadn't she'd admonish him, saying, "Don't grieve your parents. Write to them, now."

Sojourner needed money to support herself, so she did light housekeeping for several families in Battle Creek, where she now lived. Since emancipation, Sojourner had wanted to contribute more to the war effort, and, secretly, she wanted to meet President Lincoln.

Then one day in the spring of 1864, Sojourner was busy doing laundry. "I've got to hurry with this washing," she said, matter-of-factly. When asked why, she answered, "I'm leaving for Washington this afternoon. I'm going down there to advise the president."

Sammy, of course, went with her. All along the way, Sojourner stopped and visited with friends and relations, and when asked, she gave speeches. At last she and Sammy reached the nation's Capitol. When she saw the flag, she whispered to him, "No more scars and stripes, just stars and stripes for all God's children."

Parts of Washington, D.C., reminded Sojourner of the Five Point district in New York. The streets were filled with slaves who had poured into Washington after freedom. They lived in unhealthy conditions, surrounded by filth and despair. Sojourner's heart went out to them, and in her own way she helped whenever she could.

Freeing the slaves had created yet another problem: What to do with millions of people who had no education, no money, and limited skills. Congress had set aside appropriations for the establishment of the Freedman's Bureau, designed to help former slaves make the transition from slavery to freedom. Sojourner hoped there might be some job she could do for the Bureau.

When Sojourner heard that her good friend Josephine Griffing was in Washington as the local agent of the National Freedman's Relief Association, she went to her right away. Sojourner expressed her concern about the condition of the newly freed slaves. "I know just the place for you," Josephine said. "Freedman's Village."

Freedman's Village, set up by the army, was constructed as a model village. The neat cottages were a great improvement over the shacks the slaves had lived in during slavery. Sojourner later learned that the village was located on General Robert E. Lee's old estate in Arlington, Virginia, just outside Washington.

Sojourner and Sammy moved into the village. In November, she dictated a letter to her friend Amy Post in Rochester:

I am at Freedman's Village. . . . I judge it is the will of both God and the people that I should remain. Ask Mr. Oliver Johnson to please send me The Standard while I'm here, as many of the colored people like to hear what is going on and to know what is being done for them. Sammy, my grandson, reads for them.

*   *   *

Moving about like a woman half her age, Sojourner helped the women in the Village learn how to clean, sew, comb hair, and take care of their children. She sent her grandson Sammy to the Village school and encouraged mothers to send theirs, and even to attend adult classes.

One day she found a group of women huddled together frightened and crying. White men had stolen their children and made them work without pay. "Fight the robbers!" Sojourner said forcefully. "You're free now. Don't let anyone treat you like slaves."

Remembering how she'd used the law to get Peter back from Gedney, Sojourner helped the women use the law to get their children back.

One of the white men, who was from Maryland, tried to intimidate Sojourner with threats. "Old woman, stay out of our affairs, or we'll put you in jail."

The seasoned warrior didn't budge. "If you try anything like that, I shall make the United States rock like a cradle." The men left her alone and stopped raiding the Freedman's Village and stealing children.

Sojourner had been in Washington several months and she still hadn't gotten a chance to meet President Lincoln. Then on Saturday October 29, 1864, she was told that her friends had arranged for her to meet the president.

Sojourner had planned to speak with him about bettering the condition of former slaves. But, when she was introduced to the president, she looked at his weary face. His shoulders seemed to sag with the heavy burden they carried. Sojourner's heart was moved with great sadness for the man who had freed her people. She decided not to add still another complaint to his load. Instead she kept the conversation light.

"I never heard of you before you were talked of for president," she said.

The president smiled. "Well, I heard of you, years and years before I even thought of being president. Your name was well-known in the Middle West." He showed her around his office, pointing out a Bible a group of Baltimore blacks had presented to him. She held it in her hands and traced the big gold letters — THE BIBLE — with her finger. Although she couldn't read it, she knew the words in it by heart.

Remembering one of her favorite Bible stories, she reminded President Lincoln that he was like Daniel in the lion's den, but with God on his side he'd win, just like Daniel.

Then, she said that, in her opinion, he was the best president the country had ever had. But Lincoln suggested that Washington, Jefferson, and Adams were the greatest and not him. "They may have been good to others, but they neglected to do anything for my race. Washington had a good name, but his name didn't reach to us."

When it was time to leave, Sojourner asked him to sign her "Book of Life." Sojourner's "Book of Life" was a combination scrapbook and autograph book. In it, she collected the signatures of great people she'd met and respected. She also kept personal letters and newspaper clippings inside it. Everywhere that Sojourner went, she took her "Book of Life" along.

She watched with pride as Lincoln wrote:

For Aunty Sojourner Truth

And signed it

A. Lincoln
October 29, 1864

Later, "Aunty" and "Uncle" became terms elderly black women and men resented. At the time of Lincoln's autograph it was a term of endearment. General William T. Sherman was affectionately called "Uncle Billy," and General Robert E. Lee's soldier's called him "Uncle Bobby."

Sojourner was still working at the Freedman's Village when General Robert E. Lee surrendered to General Ulysses S. Grant at Appomattox Courthouse in Virginia on April 9, 1865. For all practical purposes the war was over. More than half a million people were dead.

Six days later, President Lincoln's name was added to the list of victims. A freezing drizzle fell steadily the morning it was announced that Lincoln had been assassinated while attending a play at Ford's Theater. Lincoln had been shot by an actor, John Wilkes Booth, who was later caught. After the shooting, Lincoln was taken to the home of William Peterson at 453 Tenth Street, but he died at 7:22 A.M.

Secretary of State William Seward was stabbed that same evening in a separate incident, but he survived. Vice-President Andrew Johnson became president of the United States.

Thousands of people, including Sojourner and Sammy, passed through the East Room of the White House where Lincoln's body lay in state. Sojourner looked for the last time at the president

A painting of Sojourner Truth and President Abraham Lincoln by the artist Frank Courter. Courter, who created this work after Truth's death, had Diana Corbin, Truth's daughter, pose for the painting.

who would be remembered simply as "the Emancipator."

Back at Freedman's Village, Sojourner spent hours trying to convince the former slaves that Lincoln's death didn't mean re-enslavement, and that Vice-President Johnson, although he was from Tennessee, couldn't turn back the clock. But even Sojourner wasn't as sure about the future as she tried to sound.

In the summer of 1865, Sojourner met with President Andrew Johnson. "Please be seated, Mrs. Truth," said the president.

"Sit down yourself, Mr. President," said Sojourner. "I'm used to standing because I've been lecturing for many years." She shared her concerns and the problems her people faced, based on firsthand information from Freedman's Village. The president listened politely, but he made no commitment. Although she had her "Book of Life" with her that day, Sojourner left without asking President Johnson to sign it. Whether it was an oversight or intentional is not known and she never explained it.

Not too long after her visit with Johnson, the War Department assigned Sojourner to work at the Freedman's Hospital. She was needed to help "promote order, cleanliness, industry, and virtue among the patients." Although she was seventy years old, she accepted the position. Her booming voice could be heard resounding through the corridors, "Be clean! Be clean!"

Since Sammy was helping out at the Freedman's School, he and Sojourner continued to stay in Freedman's Village. He also kept in touch with the family back in Battle Creek. By then, Sojourner's grandson James had returned home safely, after being taken prisoner during a battle. To get to and from her work, Sojourner often walked, but one day she decided to take a streetcar.

Three cars passed without stopping. As the fourth car passed, she yelled out, "I want to ride! Stop! I want to ride!" Her screams stopped traffic and finally the streetcar. After she climbed on board, the conductor threatened her, called her names, and forced her to sit in a segregated — Jim Crow — section, a section especially for blacks. Sojourner was furious!

A few days later, she and a white friend, Mrs. Laura Haviland, were getting on a streetcar together. Sojourner stepped ahead of her friend. The conductor snatched Sojourner out of the way. "Let the lady on before you," he said sharply.

"I'm a lady, too," Sojourner snapped back. The conductor pushed Sojourner. "Get off!" he yelled.

Mrs. Haviland stopped the man. "Don't put her out," she asked.

"Does she belong to you?" the conductor asked angrily.

"No," answered Mrs. Haviland. "She belongs to humanity."

"Then take her and go!" The conductor slammed Sojourner against the door and dislocated her shoulder. Little did he know he had tangled with the wrong person. Sojourner sued for assault and battery, and won. The conductor was fired! In the future, conductors behaved differently, stopping to pick up passengers regardless of color. It was final victory for an old warrior.

But the victory was short-lived. Soon, laws were passed making it illegal for blacks and whites to ride together. These "Jim Crow" laws, as they were called, stayed in force until the modern civil rights movement.

Meanwhile, Sojourner was ready to take on still another project. Blacks had worked the land for 200 years and they had nothing to show for their efforts. All they knew how to do was farm. Crowding rural people into large cities only compounded the problems. Land, she decided, was the answer.

Sojourner began talking up the idea about a land-grant program for slave families. Since farming is what they knew, then why not provide them with a way to become productive, self-sufficient citizens?

Congressional reaction to the passage of the Thirteenth Amendment abolishing slavery.

Chapter 10
The Last Cause

For years, abolitionists and women's rights activists had worked together, supporting each other's causes. When the Fifteenth Amendment was passed in 1868, black men were given the right to vote, but women were excluded. "The right of citizens of the United States to vote shall not be denied or abridged by the United States or by any state on account of race, color, or previous condition of servitude."

Women abolitionists felt betrayed by black men who had benefited from their efforts, but then seemingly deserted them. Even Frederick Douglass, who had been the first to back women's suffrage, said, "this hour belongs to the Negro." To this Elizabeth Cady Stanton retorted: "My question is this: Do you believe the African race is composed entirely of males?"

The argument even divided women into two camps. The National Woman Suffrage Association (NWSA), founded in 1869 by Elizabeth Cady Stanton and Susan B. Anthony, devoted its efforts to women's suffrage through constitutional amendment. The American Woman Suffrage Association (AWSA), founded a few months later by Lucy Stone and Henry Blackwell, believed women's suffrage was best achieved through state actions.

The battle lines were drawn and each side looked for allies among the former women abolitionists. Since Sojourner had always championed women's suffrage, Anthony wrote Sojourner a letter with a petition listing demands for women's rights and asked her to sign it. Sojourner responded:

> *There is a great stir about colored men getting their rights, but not a word about the colored women; and if colored men get their rights, and not colored women theirs, you see the colored men will be masters over the women, and it will be just as bad as it was before. So I am for keeping the thing going while things are stirring; because if we wait till it is still, it will take a great while to get it going again.*

Her prophesy was accurate. The women's suffrage movement lost momentum in the coming years. Anthony, Stanton, Stone, Truth, and others died before women finally won the right to vote in 1919.

* * *

A famous editor, Theodore Tilton, wanted to write Sojourner's life story. She answered in typical Sojourner fashion: "I am not ready to be writ up yet, for I have still lots to accomplish." And she did!

Although Sojourner was over seventy, she took up one more cause. In addition to fighting for equal rights for women, she worked for government-sponsored black homesteads out West. She argued that blacks had been forced to work with no profit from their own labor, yet no slave had ever been compensated. It was too late to pay back with money, but by setting aside land for each slave — "Twenty acres and a mule" — the government, in her opinion, could pay the dept in full.

Her job at the Freedman's Hospital had ended, so she and Sammy traveled, lecturing for equal rights for women and newly freed blacks. She returned to Washington, D.C., and visited the newly elected President Ulysses S. Grant on March 31, 1870. She hoped to gain support for her land-grant proposal.

Sojourner didn't have the conversation between Grant and herself recorded, but they seemingly parted on good terms, and he signed her "Book of Life." She also endorsed him for re-election for his second term.

But when the help she expected from Grant was not forthcoming, Sojourner took her petition to

Congress. Arriving at the Capitol building one morning dressed in her usual white cap, gray dress, and white shawl, she was a striking figure of poise. She addressed a group of senators.

"We have been a source of wealth to this republic," she said, eloquently defending her position.

Our labor supplied the country with cotton, until villages and cities dotted the enterprising North for its manufacture — and furnished employment and support for a multitude, thereby becoming a revenue to the government. . . . Our nerves and sinews, our tears and blood have been sacrificed on the altar of this nation's avarice. Our unpaid labor had been a stepping stone to its financial success. Some of its dividends must surely be ours.

A reporter wrote:

It was an hour not soon to be forgotten. It was refreshing, but also strange, to see a woman born in the shackles of slavery now treated to a reception by senators in a marble room. A decade ago she would have been spurned from its outer corridor by the lowest menial. . . . Truly, the spirit of progress is abroad in the land!

Fourteen senators signed Sojourner's "Book of Life," even though they weren't supportive of her land-grant proposal. However, Senator Charles Sumner of Massachusetts took more than a casual interest in Truth's ideas. He promised to sponsor a bill if she could show that there was wide-spread support for such a plan. Sojourner had the following petition drawn up:

TO THE SENATE AND HOUSE
OF REPRESENTATIVES,
In Congress Assembled:

Whereas, from the faithful and earnest representations of Sojourner Truth (who has personally investigated the matter) we believe that the freed colored people in and about Washington, dependent upon government for support, would be greatly benefited and might become useful citizens by being placed in a position to support themselves;

We, the undersigned, therefore earnestly request your honorable body to set apart for them a portion of the public land in the West and erect buildings thereon for the aged and infirm, and otherwise legislate so as to secure the desired results.

FREE LECTURE!

SOJOURNER TRUTH,

Who has been a slave in the State of New York, and who has been a Lecturer for the last twenty-three years, whose characteristics have been so vividly portrayed by Mrs. Harriet Beecher Stowe, as the African Sybil, will deliver a lecture upon the present issues of the day,

At   On

And will give her experience as a Slave mother and religious woman. She comes highly recommended as a public Speaker, having the approval of many thousands who have heard her earnest appeals, among whom are Wendell Phillips, Wm. Lloyd Garrison, and other distinguished men of the nation.

☞ **At the close of her discourse she will offer for sale her photograph and a few of her choice songs.**

This handbill marking one of Truth's many lectures on the abolitionist circuit is shown here with a vintage photograph.

Then, once again, Sojourner Truth set out on a journey to get her petition signed. Sammy traveled with her, and another grandson had also joined them.

On January 1, 1871, the eighth anniversary of the Emancipation Proclamation, the old warrior celebrated at Tremont Hall in Boston. She spoke about beginning life in the cellar, the beatings with a rod, and other indignities she had endured during slavery.

Now some people say, "Let the blacks take care of themselves." But you've taken everything away from them. They don't have anything left! I say, get the black people out of Washington! Get them off the government! Get the old people out and build them homes in the West, where they can feed themselves. Lift up those people and put them there. Teach them to read part of the time and teach them to work the other part of the time. Do that, and they will soon be a people among you. That is my commission!

People signed her petition gladly, even those who opposed the proposal at first. Once they heard her speak, they were convinced.

She was in Massachusetts when she received a letter from her friend Olive Gilbert, the woman

who had written her autobiography while they
were at Northampton, Massachusetts.

Dear Sojourner:
My dear friend. A line from my brother received
this afternoon, speaks of your being at Vineland,
so I must send you a few lines to say how much
pleased I was to hear from you through friend
Amy Post of Rochester, New York. . . . I get a
glimpse of you often through the papers, which
falls upon my spirit like bright rays from the sun.
. . . I rejoice and am proud that you can make
your power felt with so little book-education.

Sojourner went to visit Olive, who helped Sojourner gather more signatures for her petition.

Returning to Washington a year later with thousands of signatures, she hurried to Sumner's office,
only to be told by his secretary that the great
senator had recently died. No other person would
help her with the cause. Gone were all of Sojourner's hopes for ever getting her plan introduced
as a bill.

At last she decided it was time to go home —
home to Michigan. She missed Battle Creek, but
more importantly Sammy was ill. It didn't seem
serious at first, but his fever got worse and so did
his cough. He died in February 1875. He hadn't
had his twenty-fifth birthday yet. It was worse than

Sojourner Truth's daughter, Diana Corbin.

losing Peter, because Sammy had been such a good and faithful companion. She never stopped mourning for him.

No matter what she did, Sojourner couldn't work away the hurt. She missed Sammy terribly, and without him she felt handicapped, because he had read to her, taken care of all her correspondence, and looked after her affairs.

She wrote to her family in Battle Creek that she was on the way home to die. But she outlived her grandson by nine years. In 1878 she even went out on a speaking tour covering thirty-six different towns in Michigan. And, at eighty-one, she was one of three Michigan delegates to the Woman's Rights Convention in Rochester. After a gruelling trip to Kansas, where she spoke to newly freed slaves who were planning to homestead, Sojourner did come home for good.

She returned to Battle Creek, physically spent. Dr. John Harvey Kellogg, director of the Battle Creek Sanitarium, admitted her, because she was near death. In the fall of 1883, he wrote to her friend Josephine, "Her illness is very severe and causes her great pain. All hope is now given up of a restoration to health."

"I'm going home like a shooting star," she told her family and friends. Then at 3:00 A.M. on the morning of November 26, 1883, Sojourner Truth died at age eighty-six. She was eulogized as a dynamic woman with strength, integrity, poise, and

Sojourner Truth's gravesite in Battle Creek, Michigan.

wit. After her funeral, she was buried at Oak Hill
Cemetery near her grandson Sammy.

A reporter described that last scene: "The long
line of carriages, the hearse with its black plumes,
the people — all so motionless — the cloudless
sky, the great round, red sun lying low on the
horizon. . . ." And, as the coffin was lowered into
the ground, the sun set.

At the time of her death, a Battle Creek paper
stated: "This country has lost one of its most re-
markable personages."

But Sojourner is not really lost to us.

Whenever people speak out against injustice
and scorn oppression, Sojourner Truth is in their
midst. Wherever people are working to make conditions better for the weak and downtrodden, Sojourner is there rejoicing. Whoever believes in
equality, freedom, and justice keeps the spirit of
Sojourner Truth alive and well.

More About the People
Sojourner Truth Knew

RICHARD ALLEN
(1760–1831)

Richard Allen was born a slave in Delaware in 1760. He became a Methodist minister and converted his master. Later Allen bought his freedom and, in 1786, he settled in Philadelphia. He converted many African-Americans to the Methodist faith, all of whom joined the intergrated St. George's Methodist Church.

In 1787, tension between blacks and whites at St. George's began to increase. Allen proposed that African-Americans form their own church. He formed the Free African Society, which was dedicated to self-improvement and advancement of blacks. Later that same year, St. George's began to segregate blacks by putting them in the gallery of the church. Allen and Absalom Jones led an exodus of blacks from St. George's. While Jones started a church that stayed within the Methodist church, Allen started the first African Methodist American Church, Bethal African Methodist Episcopal (AME) Church.

Allen was ordained the first bishop of the AME Church in 1799. In 1816, Allen was able to win complete separation from the Protestant Episcopal Church and legally established the AME Church.

SUSAN B. ANTHONY
(1820–1906)

In February 1820, Susan Anthony was born in Adams, Massachusetts. Her father, Daniel, was a Quaker abolitionist and cotton manufacturer. Susan, a very intelligent child, learned to read and write at the age of three. In 1826, the family moved from Massachusetts to Battenville, New York.

After teaching for a while, Anthony joined Elizabeth Cady Stanton and Amelia Bloomer in a campaign to gain women's rights. Anthony also worked as an abolitionist.

From 1856 to 1861 she served as an agent of the American Anti-Slavery Society. After slavery was abolished, Anthony demanded that women be granted the same rights black men were given under the Fourteenth and Fifteenth Amendments to the U.S. Constitution.

In 1872, to test the Fourteenth Amendment, she voted

in the presidential election. She was arrested and fined. She refused to pay the fine, but the case was dropped.

She, along with her associates Stanton and Matilda Joslyn Gage, compiled and published *The History of Woman Suffrage*. In 1888 Anthony organized the International Council of Women and in 1904 the International Woman Suffrage Alliance. She was acclaimed worldwide for her great contribution to women's suffrage. Susan B. Anthony died on March 13, 1906, in Rochester, New York. She did not live long enough to see women win the right to vote in 1919.

JOHN BROWN
(1800–1859)

John Brown was born on May 9, 1800, in Torrington, Connecticut. Brown was one of the most militant of the abolitionists. His hatred of slavery, fueled by the horrors he heard while living in a black settlement in upstate New York, led him and five of his sons to move to Kansas in 1855. He led several raids against pro-slavery strongholds in Kansas. After the city of Lawrence was attacked by pro-slavery forces in 1856, Brown led a counterattack on the small village on the Pottawatomie Creek. Five men from the settlement were killed.

Brown announced in Chatham, Ontario (Canada), that

he was setting up an anti-slavery stronghold in the mountains of Virginia and Maryland, from which attacks against selected targets in the southern United States could be conducted. He received support from several abolitionists, including Gerrit Smith.

On the night of October 16, 1859, Brown and twenty-one men attacked the armory at Harpers Ferry and rounded up sixty men from the area as hostages. Government forces, headed by Colonel Robert E. Lee, attacked the armory, killing ten men — two of whom were Brown's sons. Brown survived the attack but was wounded. He was charged with murder and treason and was hanged on December 2, 1859. Brown's actions heightened the tension between Northern abolitionists and Southern slave owners.

FREDERICK DOUGLASS
(Circa 1817–1895)

Frederick Douglass was born in Tuckahoe, Maryland, in 1817. Douglass lived eight years in Baltimore, serving as a houseboy for Hugh and Sophia Auld. There, Frederick learned to read and write just enough to complete his education on his own. He was sent back to a plantation in rural Maryland where he was beaten in order to break his spirit and make him more docile. But Frederick kept his spirit alive by dreaming of the day he would be a free man.

That day finally came in 1837, when he made his way to Baltimore and then New York. He sent for Anna Murray, a free black woman, who came to New York, where they were married in 1837.

Douglass, without any formal education, became an articulate spokesman for the abolitionist movement. He edited a newspaper, *The North Star*, and published editorials in other journals. His autobiography, *Narrative of Frederick Douglass*, published in 1845, made him a fugitive again, so he left the country and lived in England for several years. His friends in England bought his freedom, so he was able to return to America and continue his work. During the Civil War, Douglass helped recruit blacks to serve in the Union Army.

After the war, he settled in Anacostia, District of Columbia. There he served in a variety of positions under several presidents. Douglass died in his home in 1895.

WILLIAM LLOYD GARRISON
(1805–1879)

William Lloyd Garrison was born on October 11, 1805, in Newburyport, Massachusetts. Garrison joined the abolitionist movement at the age of twenty-three. He served as editor of many journals, including the *Journal of the Times* and the *National Philanthropist*. In 1829 he worked as co-editor on the *Genius of Universal Emancipation.* Garrison was sent to prison in 1829 for his position on slavery, but was released a few months later in 1830.

Garrison created *The Liberator* in 1830, which established him as a leading advocate in the anti-slavery movement. In 1833, he helped start the American Anti-Slavery Society, but was criticized because he wanted to include women in the society. Although he was opposed to violence, he praised John Brown's raid on Harpers Ferry as "God's method of dealing retribution on the head of the tyrant."

Garrison supported Lincoln, and the Civil War as well — believing it was the only means by which slaves could be freed. He quit as president of the American Anti-Slavery Society in 1864, declaring that his time as an abolitionist had ended. Garrison continued to support the women's movement, voters' rights, civil rights, and the temperance movement. He died on May 24, 1879, in New York City.

JOHN JAY
(1745–1829)

John Jay was born on December 12, 1745, in Bedford, New York. Jay, a lawyer, was first a British loyalist and then one of the nation's founders. He became the first Chief Justice of the Supreme Court from 1789 to 1795.

In 1794, Jay was sent to England by President George Washington to settle the grievances between England and the United States. The Jay Treaty was signed November 19, 1794. It settled major problems between the two countries and helped promote economic prosperity. Jay also was an early opponent of slavery and supported abolition, much to the aggravation of his Southern colleagues.

Jay became Governor of New York in 1795, but he retired in 1801. John Jay spent the next twenty-seven years on his farm in rural New York State and died on May 17, 1829.

Lucretia Mott
(1793–1880)

Lucretia Coffin Mott was born on January 3, 1793, in Nantucket, Massachusetts. Mott, along with Elizabeth Stanton, helped found the Women's Rights Movement in America.

Mott, a Quaker, attended the Friends' boarding school in Poughkeepsie, New York. By age fifteen she was a teacher. She also took an interest in the rights of women, when she found out that she earned only half the wages male teachers were given at the school.

In 1811, Lucretia Coffin married James Mott, also a teacher at the same school. The couple moved to Philadelphia and took part in the anti-slavery movement there. In 1850, when a stricter Fugitive Slave Act was passed, the

Motts used their home as a station on the Underground
Railroad, an escape route slaves used.

In 1848 Mott helped organize the Women's Rights Convention in Seneca Falls, New York. Mott wrote articles and
lectured widely. She was elected president of the conference
in 1852. She worked consistently and tirelessly for the issue
of women's rights until her death on November 11, 1880.

WENDELL
PHILLIPS
(1811–1884)

Wendell Phillips was born on November 29, 1811, in Boston. Phillips graduated from Harvard Law School, but gave
up a life of status and wealth in order to join the anti-
slavery movement.

He worked closely with his friend, the abolitionist William Lloyd Garrison. Phillips contributed to the anti-slavery
campaign by writing pamphlets and editorials in Garrison's
newspaper, *The Liberator*. He first spoke publicly on December 8, 1837, at a gathering in Boston protesting the
death of Elijah Lovejoy, a newspaper owner and abolitionist
who had been murdered in Alton, Illinois. His passionate
speech and fiery spirit led many to say that he should be
the leading speaker for the abolitionist movement. Both

Phillips and Garrison denounced the Constitution because it upheld slavery. Phillips went a step further and recommended that the South should be expelled from the Union until slavery was abolished. After the Emancipation Proclamation, Phillips worked to better the lives of the newly freed men and women. After the war ended, Phillips worked for the women's movement, civil rights, voters' rights, and temperance.

Wendell Phillips died February 2, 1884, in Boston.

David Ruggles
(1810–1849)

David Ruggles was born in Connecticut, in 1810. He moved to New York in 1827 to work as an abolitionist. He later became editor and publisher of the anti-slavery magazine, *The Mirror of Liberty*.

Ruggles was in poor health, but he improved after receiving hydrotherapeutic treatments. Ruggles was so impressed with the process that he studied it and later opened a hydrptherapeutic treatment center in Northampton, Massachusetts. He treated both black and white patients, including William Lloyd Garrison and Frederick Douglass, well-known abolitionist leaders.

DRED SCOTT
(Circa 1795–1858)

Dred Scott was born in Southampton County, Virginia, the slave of Peter Blow. Blow moved his family and Scott to Missouri in 1827. Through several transfers, Scott became the servant of the widow of Dr. John Emerson. She hired him out to several families in St. Louis.

In 1846, Henry Taylor Blow, the son of Peter Blow, brought a suit to court (*Scott, a Colored Man* v. *John F.A. Sandford Emerson*) claiming Scott was free because he had been moved to the free state of Illinois and the free territory of Minnesota. Was Scott legally free? The Missouri judge ruled against Scott, but the case was taken to federal court and then to the United States Supreme Court. The Supreme Court ruled in favor of Missouri. Scott was a slave and not a citizen of the United States, so his suit could not and should not have been heard. Henry Blow bought Scott in 1857 and gave him his freedom. Scott continued to live in St. Louis, working as a porter until his death in 1858.

Although Scott lost his case, it helped fan the fires of anti-slavery.

ELIZABETH STANTON
(1815–1902)

Elizabeth Cady Stanton was born on October 26, 1815, in New York City. She studied law with her father, Daniel Cady, a U.S. congressman and a New York State Supreme Court Justice. During her studies she became aware of the discrimination against women and vowed to change the system that oppressed women.

In 1840 Elizabeth Cady married Henry Brewster Stanton, but she continued her work. He helped secure the passage of a New York statute granting women property rights in a marriage. Stanton teamed up with Lucretia Mott to organize the first Woman's Rights Convention in Seneca Falls, New York. Everything went smoothly until Stanton introduced a resolution for women's suffrage. Mott was against the idea of voting rights, and eventually it led to a split in the movement.

In 1850, Stanton joined Susan B. Anthony, whose philosophy was more compatible to hers. Anthony handled the business affairs of the movement while Stanton wrote. The two finished several books together including *Revolution* and *The History of Woman Suffrage*.

Stanton died on October 26, 1902, in New York City.

LUCY
STONE
(1818–1893)

Lucy Stone was a pioneer in the women's rights movement and a big supporter of the abolitionist movement.

Ms. Stone was born in West Brookfield, Massachusetts, in August 1818. After graduation from Oberlin College, Ohio, in 1847, Stone became a lecturer for the Massachusetts Anti-Slavery Society. The society granted Stone a part of each week to lecture on women's rights and suffrage.

In 1855, Stone married Ohio abolitionist Henry Blackwell. She retained her maiden name, Stone, to protest the unequal laws of marriage. The couple lived in New Jersey for a little more than a decade, promoting the rights of women.

In 1869, Stone and her husband established the American Woman Suffrage Association. The organization's goal was to promote suffrage on the state level, while the National Woman Suffrage Association, a rival group, supported a constitutional amendment granting women equal rights. Stone helped start the *Woman's Journal*, a suffrage weekly.

Lucy Stone died on October 18, 1893, in Dorchester, Massachusetts.

Harriet Beecher Stowe
(1811–1896)

Harriet Beecher Stowe was born on June 14, 1811, in Litch-field, Connecticut. Her father, Lyman Beecher, was a famous minister. She taught school in Hartford, but moved to Cincinnati in 1832. There she taught school and socialized in literary circles. Harriet Beecher married Calvin Ellis Stowe, a clergyman and seminary professor, in 1836. He encouraged her to write.

In 1850, the Stowes moved to Brunswick, Maine, where Calvin Stowe became a professor at Bowdoin College. It was in Brunswick that Harriet wrote her most famous book, *Uncle Tom's Cabin, or Life Among the Lowly*. The book was so popular it was translated into twenty-three languages. In 1853, she published *The Key to Uncle Tom's Cabin*, which documented slavery as an abusive, inhumane system.

Because of her works against slavery, Harriet Beecher Stowe rallied Northern sentiments against Southern slave owners. When President Lincoln met her he said, "So you're the little lady who started this big war." Harriet Stowe died on July 1, 1896.

HARRIET TUBMAN
(Circa 1821–1913)

Harriet Tubman was born a slave in Dorchester County, Maryland, in 1821. The exact date is impossible to pinpoint because slave records were not kept accurately. Tubman worked as a field hand until, after marrying a free black, John Tubman, and fearing she was about to be sold, she ran away at about age twenty-five.

Later, Tubman made twenty successful trips back to the South and led more than 300 others to freedom by using a series of safe houses and routes known as the Underground Railroad. Tubman never lost one life. She became known as the "Moses" of her people. During the Civil War she served as a guide, spy, and nurse for the Union Army.

After the war she turned her attention to building and funding a nursing home for older, homeless African-Americans.

Bibliography

Andrews, William L. *Sisters of the Spirit*. Bloomington, IN: Indiana University Press, 1986.

Bernard, Jacqueline. *Journey Toward Freedom*. New York: The Feminist Press at The City University of New York, 1967 and 1990.

Claflin, Edward Beecher. *Sojourner Truth and the Struggle for Freedom*. New York: Barron's Educational Series, 1987.

Evans, Sara M. *Born for Liberty — A History of Women in America*. New York: The Free Press — A Division of Collier Macmillan, 1989.

Hoffelt, Robert O. *AME Bicentennial Hymnal*. Nashville, TN: The African Methodist Episcopal Church Press, 1984.

Hooker, Gloria. *I Shall Not Live in Vain — A Biography of Harriet Beecher Stowe*. St. Louis, MO: Concordia Publishing House, 1978.

Hooks, Bell. *Ain't I a Woman?* Boston, MA: South End Press, 1991.

Krass, Peter. *Sojourner Truth — Antislavery Activist*. New York: Chelsea House Publishers, 1988.

Lerner, Gerda (ed.). *Black Women in White America*. New York: Random House, 1973.

Lindstrom, Aletha Jane. *Sojourner Truth*. New York: Julian Messner, 1980.

Litwack, Leon, and August Meier (eds.). *Black Leaders of the Nineteenth Century*. Urbana and Chicago, IL: University of Illinois Press, 1988.

McFeely, William S. *Frederick Douglass*. New York: W. W. Norton and Company, 1991.

Ortiz, Victoria. *Sojourner Truth, A Self-Made Woman*. Philadelphia, PA: J. B. Lippincott Company, 1974.

Silber, Irwin (ed.). *Songs of the Civil War*. New York: Columbia University Press, 1960.

Stampp, Kenneth. *The Peculiar Institution — Slavery in the Ante-Bellum South*. New York: Random House, 1984.

Wayne, Bennett (ed.). *Black Crusaders for Freedom*. Champaign, IL: Garrard Publishing Company, 1974.

Index

Page references in italics indicate material in illustrations.

181

Photo Credits